Dissent and the State in Peace and War

Morton A. Kaplan

An *Essai* on the Grounds
of Public Morality

Dissent and
the State in
Peace and War

THE DUNELLEN COMPANY, INC., New York

International Standard Book Number 0-8424-0007-9.

Library of Congress Catalogue Card Number 71-125540.

Printed in the United States of America.

Contents

Preface

The passion to rebel against injustice, when it is genuine, is a rare and noble virtue. The wisdom to know how and when to do so is rarer still. Respect for political due process—the supporting structure without which substantive justice is impossible —requires wisdom. Respect for the autonomy of others requires compassion. The ability to govern others rests upon the ability to govern oneself. No man acquires these virtues in the absence of an education, whether formal or informal, that inculcates respect for them. These considerations adumbrate the concerns that led to the writing of this book.

It will be fairly obvious that most of the issues I discuss have been sucked into the vortex of the dissent to the Vietnamese War. What started as a protest against an "unjust" war broadened into an attack on "illegitimate" government, institutional racism, and the educational process. Although I reject many of the simplistic notions of the dissenters—I do not believe, for instance, that the war arises out of capitalism or that the latter produces and accounts for racism—the questions that are raised are often profound and deserve serious consideration. Thus, although I reject the oversimplified, holistic way in which many of the dissenters explain all current evils as products of "The System," and this book will reflect my effort to disentangle the various issues, the issues are intrinsically important and require serious discussion. Above all, the issues of legitimacy, dissent, and political obligation require examination. If I strongly object to the ofttimes cavalier ways in which the dissenters have raised these issues, to their neglect of moral "due process," and to their careless examination of the circumstances of governmental decisions, I agree that we owe them a debt of gratitude for bringing these issues at last into public view.

This book is an *essai*. The original French spelling is used to indicate that it attempts to explore the subject rather than to come to definitive conclusions. It attempts to get others to think about the issues rather than to present them with a set of systematic answers. It is short and selective in its topics. It is polemical but it attempts more to raise questions than to answer them. Free men have inquiring minds, and a free society permits such men to develop and to flourish. A proper educational process, for instance, is central to freedom. Yet we live in a world that is not entirely benign. Actions are not good in themselves but depend upon consequences; and these in turn may be dependent upon such distasteful subjects as bargaining styles and military ratios.

A number of the positions I take are currently unpopular in academia. I will not apologize for them. Those who disagree will do better to argue with these positions when they are well presented by their advocates than to argue with the caricatures they themselves usually present. I have not attempted to stress the usual academic liberal critique of government. These positions are well known in academia and hardly need restatement. Although the academic liberals are often accurately and helpfully critical of governmental hypocrisy or corruption, they are at least as often self-serving and guilty of double standards. A minor purpose of this book is to puncture the self-serving hypocrisies and pomposities of the common "academic intellectual" position.

Some may see my position as conservative, but it is really radical in the root sense. It rejects facile liberalism; it dismisses the idea of the state or of the educational process as neutral. Popular "radicalism" is dismissed as morally corrupt. Conservative positions are seen as inadequate from the standpoint of justice in a changing and increasingly rich world. However inadequately it does so, this *essai* attempts to hint at a conception of the state, of education, and of citizen participation adequate to the world we live in and grounded in fundamental principles of political philosophy.

The last chapter, reprinted from *Ethics,* introduces its perspectives from a somewhat more professional standpoint than do previous chapters. This, however, does not mean that the issues raised in the earlier chapters are less important philosophically than those of the last chapter. The philosophical issues raised in this book—in particular, those related to the issue of human freedom, that is, of autonomous self-control—are derived from the philosophy of systemic pragmaticism, the foundations of which are presented in *Macropolitics*.[1] My position that the choices among values are decidable and that moral rules rather than merely act-utilitarian decisions[2] are required in society is also developed in that book.[3]

A reader asserted that he disagreed with the "attitudes" underlying this book. The values underlying it are clear. I believe that human beings should live in a society that permits them to become autonomous and self-directing. The prisoner freed after 30 years may flee back to the security of his jail, but his desire to return does not make the jail a desirable social institution. He has been crippled by his life experiences. I believe that institutions that cripple human beings are bad and that they are even worse if they produce acceptance of the crippling conditions. I do not believe that any society yet is a free society or that there are many autonomous human beings. But some societies contain the potentiality for future human freedom. I think these societies, despite their current defects, need to be preserved, and that a world hostile to them and to their values would be evil. I believe such societies can be preserved only by dedication and intelligence. If these are the values from which people dissent, then I wish they would be clear about it. If, on the other hand, they disagree on instrumentalities for the achieving of these values, a constructive dialogue should be possible. In that case, the disagreement is not over "attitudes" but over empirical estimates of situations and their interpretation and of the consequences of alternative kinds of interventions.

I have stated that my objective in this small book is more to raise questions than to answer them. The discussion in Chapter 3 of the limitation of principles exemplifies this. If no principle is directly applicable to a set of circumstances (I do not intend to deny that sometimes principles must be applied as the best rule of thumb under conditions of gross uncertainty), then none of the perspectives in this section of the book is applicable to any particular set of circumstances without examination and qualification, except for such methodological perspectives as that of the limitation of all principles. Perspectives are useful as first approximations or as orientations rather than as answers to questions.

Except for the purely methodological perspectives, all the perspectives offered rest on substantive beliefs concerning the real world. Some of these underlying assumptions are so minimal and commonsensical that most reflective individuals would accept them in the absence of a convincing demonstration to the contrary. Others are clearly polemical and rest on minimal evidence. The program for the restructuring of the public schools obviously is highly controversial. I am sure that many intelligent scholars would seriously question it. Such polemical assertions require careful analysis and thorough investigation. I hope that my readers will neither accept nor reject such propositions uncritically but instead will turn their minds to the serious questions of political education they raise. If one accepts the failure of current public education as a fact, then it is urgent to have a radical examination of the issues. In such circumstances, a polemic can be enlightening, providing that one is aware that it is a deliberate device.

Many of the perspectives are in a no-man's-land between those that do and those that do not make major substantive assumptions. The reader should be alert to this problem. It is my hope that he will not confuse the character of the issues raised with the details of the assumptions that I make.

It has been mentioned that many decisions are made under circumstances of gross uncertainty. The first professional article that I published atempted to raise this issue in a serious way, to relate it to the problem of values and to the problem of interpreting the possible motivations and predicting the future behavior of others.[4] In this period, during the height of the Cold War, I took the occasion to attack uncritical Cold War interpretations of Soviet policy—and to point out that Soviet policy might change after Stalin's impending death—as I have since attacked equally dogmatic détente interpretations of Soviet behavior. Such dogmatisms have no place in scholarly discourse or in education.

To state that dogmatic intepretations have no place in education does not imply, however, that they are never functional in statecraft. Statesmen at times do have to act under conditions of major uncertainty. Sometimes they must act as if a particular interpretation was true. Hitler, unlike the German generals, did take the measure of the British—or of Chamberlain. He did not properly take the measure of the Yugoslavs in 1941 or of Mussolini prior to his invasion of Greece. The Russians did take the measure of the Czechoslovaks in 1968, at least in the sense of recognizing that they would not fight. They have also misjudged the political will of the Czechoslovaks; how badly they have done so or what consequences this will have we do not yet know. Statesmen necessarily rest decisions at least partly on intuition. Yet it appears reasonable to assert that they ought to be capable of distinguishing between a ground assumed for purposes of action and a confirmed condition or fact. They ought to know in general when gambles are required and when prudence is a virtue. These are questions I explore elsewhere in greater detail;[5] they are raised in more general form in this book.

This book contains three distinctive but related kinds of materials. There is an abstract discussion of the principles of obligation and legitimacy in a democracy. This occurs primarily, but not exclusively, in Chapters 2, 3, and 4, and at times is illustrated by materials from current controversies. A second type of material involves discussion of some of the most pressing moral problems of our time—problems that arise out of conditions of the world and that require illumination within that context. The processes of education, the governance of the university, the defects of capitalism and of purely instrumental relationships, and the treatment of minorities, among others, fall within this category. Rejections of legitimacy can be understood in part only within the framework of these moral crises; abstract discussions of legitimacy, of obligation, and of the role of dissent may pale into pure abstraction if these moral problems are not at least discussed. A third category of materials represents an attempt briefly to say something about the nature of the world we live in, the problems of bargaining with adversaries whose goals and values differ from ours, the choices made available by the character of international politics, and the kind of world we might work to create. Although these materials are less directly relevant to the themes of political legitimacy and of political obligation, they are of great indirect importance. Discussion of them is useful to indicate how much of what has been transformed into a debate over principles may stem from a misunderstanding of conditions in the world and of the consequences of alternative decisions. If this is so, much of the temper of current dissent is misplaced. Since Chapters 5, 6, and 7 are largely characterized by materials of this last kind, I will return to this theme at the beginning of Chapter 5.

All three types of material are required to understand the principles that ought to govern dissent and the extent to which some of the extreme currents of contemporary dissent may rest on a refusal to consider the real choices confronting us—a refusal which for that reason may itself be contrary to the requirements of political morality. It is this last consideration, which is treated in the first and last chapters of the book, that brings harmony to the discussion and that relates education—the process of training autonomous minds—to political morality. The romantic rejection of real choices is itself a philosophical mistake and a moral failure.

Man may or may not be a political animal. If, however, he fails to consider moral and political questions seriously, he may reduce himself and his progeny to an ugly and distasteful, if not brutal, animality. Although I do not believe there is a moral design of the world, such that we get that which we deserve, I suggest that many of our failures are moral failures, at least some of which are produced by dogmatic beliefs and by self-righteousness. Those who would imprison the world within the seams of their private utopias really do not desire freedom for themselves or for others, no matter how much they bandy the term. The problems which some ignore out of apathy or selfishness, others "solve" for us or push their opposite extremes into "solving" in ways that frustrate civility and humanity.

Tragedy occurs when important values conflict recalcitrantly in a hostile world, when dilemmas of action adamantly confront us, or when *fortuna* repeatedly rolls the dice against us in a world we can at best see darkly. History produces its ironies even for those who aim modestly but justly and who understand the inevitable failures of human motivation and human understanding. Not all who act deserve compassion, however. Those who impose their idiocies on the world are merely comedians, and badly educated ones at that. Education is the key, for only the properly educated can understand, appreciate, and work toward freedom. We are what we learn to be. When we are taught poorly or when we learn poorly, we are but caricatures of human beings. The comedy then is low comedy and lies in our stumbling over small obstacles on the stage of history that the sighted can see. Such low comedy, however, is not always amusing to the actors on the stage. And if all of us are on a living stage, only the gods on their Olympian heights may find occasion for mockery.

Notes

1. Morton A. Kaplan, *Macropolitics: Essays on the Philosophy and Science of Politics* (Chicago: Aldine, 1969). See especially the lead essay, pp. 3 ff.

2. An act-utilitarian position is one that justifies an act by its consequences alone rather than by the standard of a general rule. Thus, if one weighs the act of using water during a water shortage, one considers only the costs and benefits of the particular act (not necessarily on a selfish basis) and not the value of the rule itself. It can be shown that the act-utilitarian position is self-defeating in many kinds of conditions and that society requires some moral rules that are regarded as having intrinsic value.

3. *Ibid.*, pp. 34 ff., 135 ff.

4. "An Introduction to the Strategy of Statecraft," *World Politics* (July 1952), pp. 539-576.

5. *On Historical and Political Knowing: An Inquiry Into Some Problems of Universal Law and Human Freedom* (University of Chicago Press, forthcoming in 1971).

Dissent and
the State in
Peace and War

1   Decisions by Calculation
or by Feeling?

We appear to be entering an era in which there is a strong resurgence of romanticism—an era in which human feelings and spontaneity are again being asserted against reason. Alternation between life styles appears to be a secular process and to recur fairly often in history. As the advantages of one phase of the cycle become taken for granted and as the costs imposed by it loom large, there seems to be a transition to its opposite. Whatever explanation we provide for this process—and we do not argue that it is self-contained or inexorable—it is apparently not to be exorcized merely by intellectual appeals. The process does go too deep for this, and the proponents of romanticism, in any event, are resistant by conviction to the voices of reason. It is nonetheless a legitimate intellectual endeavor to attempt to assess the validity of the claims made by proponents of the opposed life styles.

Romantic movements, whatever their guise or the era in which they appear, represent a search for authenticity. Fichte's *Addresses to the German Nation,* written in the early nineteenth century, compares the German language as an ur-language with French or Italian as derived languages and stresses the vigor and meaningful quality of original or authentic tongues. Romanticism identifies authenticity with feelings, with face-to-face groups or with tribes, with spontaneity, with joy or immediate satisfaction, and with assumed originality. In its extreme form, it represents the psychopathic type of which we speak in Chapter 8, just as the process of reason in its extreme form becomes deracinated and represents the compulsive-obsessive type. Each extreme overreacts against the other; each sets up supposedly impregnable defenses against the other. The romantic, or psychopathic, extreme denies the claims of reason, of moral principle, of delayed response. The compulsive-obsessive extreme denies the claims of the particular, the idiosyncratic, the immediate, the sensuous, the calls of the body. When Hegel, in *The Phenomenology of the Mind,* called for the union of the heart and of the mind, he was claiming that the whole man exists only in the synthesis of the two extremes.

We require an analysis that enables us to separate the claims of the contending approaches into areas or segments where they are and where they are not justified. We will not attempt to do that systematically here, but we will attempt to illustrate the way in which it might be done. Yet we cannot do this without pointing out that each of the claims contains an important element of truth. It is this element of truth and the secondary gains associated with it that help to support the strong and neurotic attachments of the various proponents to their individual pathologies.

Both the claim that one must do what one feels to be right and the claim that one must do that which has the best consequences represent striking insights into the demands of moral behavior, even though they often give rise to inconsistent prescriptions. Both the claim that one must opt out of a mad system and the claim that one has a responsibility to improve social or political life, however bad it is, represent judgments of at least limited validity. Consider the case of a mother who is told by a tyrant that all her five sons will be killed unless she selects one of the five, who alone will be allowed to live. Obviously, it is better to have one son alive than all dead. Yet how can the mother select a particular son to live? If she saves that one son, she must live with the fact that she could have saved any one of the others. The death of each of the four, whoever they are, then becomes a matter of her choice. A mother capable of that kind of choice may well be incapable of the kind of warmth and support required for the proper upbringing of children. The personality system is apparently not so flexible that one can apply the appropriate behavior in the normal situations of life and then switch its programming for the extreme occasions of the type cited above. In situations of this kind, it is credible, although perhaps arguable, that mothers must opt out of such situations in the sense that they must refuse to make these kinds of choices. To argue that the mother in this circumstance must calculate the consequences and make a utilitarian decision may be to argue that she must opt for madness, that she must violate her most deeply held maternal instincts.

Yet consider the case of a mother whose child becomes a rapist and murderer. Must she turn him in to the police? Obviously doing so, unless she is a callous and deracinated person, will be a painful and costly decision. Yet such a decision can be sanctioned by the general mores of the society. It need not be inconsistent with the kind of warm and supportive role a mother is expected to perform. Whereas in the first case she is confronted with the arbitrary demand of a tyrant who lacks legitimacy, in the second case the son has brought his punishment upon himself by his own execrable behavior. To fail to turn the son in is inconsistent with the moral obligations of the parent. Even though this type of moral obligation involves, not spontaneous face-to-face relations, but a relationship to an abstract moral code, it affects people too—and in the most important and most pervasive ways—through its effects upon the style of life in the community. Where such mediated obligations to the larger society are not accepted by people, one gets the kind of psychopathic social behavior that Edward C. Banfield found in a southern Italian town and described in his book *The Moral Basis of a Backward Society*.[1]

Some of the less extreme romantics, however, might argue that they often mediate their actions in terms of implicit rules that they feel to be right. For instance, they might argue that it is bad to drop bombs on people and that they refuse to calculate the consequences if they are asked to drop bombs on people. They might take the position that a system that requires such actions is mad and that sane people can only opt out. Banfield's small-town Italian might argue that he also acts for reasons he feels to be right—to protect a relative, to get food for the family, or so forth—and that in any event the larger system is rotten. Yet we cannot examine these claims unless we examine the consequences of the implicit rules that are advocated. Their goodness, contrary to what many believe, is often not evident upon mere inspection.

The supporters of conscience often overlook the social, the political, or the organizational context within which conscience is to be employed. Some of them, for instance, attempt to convince army officers that they should behave entirely according to conscience and they cite the Nuremberg trials approvingly. Yet imagine the situation if all SAC officers followed their conscience. There might be some who would attempt to fly planes over the Soviet Union and to drop nuclear weapons or to set off a Minuteman against presidential orders, thus starting a nuclear war. There might be others who would refuse to participate in a decision for a pre-emptive strike, thus ensuring an ineffective strike and thereby producing the worst of all possible worlds.

The distinction between conscience and feeling—that is, between abstract rule and felt right—is often confused. Thus, in the example given above, the proponents of conscience are usually those who operate on felt "rightness" rather than those who operate on abstract and unqualified principles. It is obsessive conscience—that is, conscience based on abstract rule—that produces deracination. Both types of claim to conscience, however, are alike in failing to give sufficient weight to the context within which decisions are made.

We cannot begin to analyze most political decisions until we examine the relations between individual decisions, the social systems and subsystems within which they operate, and the environmental conditions that constrain choice. The particularistic decisions of Banfield's Italians reinforce an immoral social system; yet the individual acting alone cannot change the system. Sometimes the actions of a great nation can change the international system for better or for worse. Yet the Italian who acts according to a universalistic morality in Banfield's case will probably injure only himself and his family, whereas so-called "good" behavior by a great state in the international system may change the entire system for the worse and injure other nations as well. On the other hand, there may be occasions on which particular interventions can better the system. These are not questions that are decidable in general. Only analysis can help to provide the answers.

If we examine the differences between those cases where calculations are desirable and those where they are not, we can discover a meta-analytical level where calculations are appropriate for both. At this metalevel we can calculate concerning the cases in which calculations are appropriate and those in which they are not.[2] If, for instance, we ask whether we want to live in the kind of world in which mothers will be able to respond to the demands of tyrants by making utilitarian calculations, the answer is palpably negative. If we do not live in such a world, we will not willingly opt to enter it. Therefore it is appropriate that mothers be acculturated to respond in warm, supportive, diffuse, and particularistic ways to their children. (Were we, however, to live in a situation of such tyranny that situations of the type depicted earlier arose constantly, the moral problem would become hideous.) On the other hand, unless we want to find ourselves in the situation of Banfield's village, then we want parents who are capable of behaving with social responsibility when their children become threats to the society. In this case, even if we do not wish to be too harsh on parents who fail to behave with social responsibility, we surely do not wish to exculpate them. Human personality systems apparently can cope with these distinctions. Properly differentiated behavior is possible and socially desirable. Spontaneity and universal norm-oriented behavior can coexist.

When a society undergoes great social transitions such that the appropriate style of principled behavior changes, the way is open for tragedy. The social changes associated with the rise of the *demes* in ancient Greece are recorded in the poems of Hesiod; the tragedy *Antigone* rests in part on the conflicting obligations of kinship and of citizenship.

In substance, one can reason both about where one ought to reason and about where one ought not to reason. Constant utilitarian calculations are obviously inappropriate within a marriage. If a husband or wife were to calculate every day whether

he or she could change partners for the better, it would be inconsistent with the maintenance of the marriage. Obviously
if grievances rise to a high enough level, then calculations become
necessary. Yet the grievances must be quite large before the
process of calculation begins, if the marriage is to be successful.
On the other hand, constant utilitarian calculations are obviously
much more appropriate in business establishments, although perhaps even here the extreme case would be dysfunctional. The
more the businessman acts out of friendship rather than out of
calculation, the more he reduces his chances for survival. If, on
the other hand, the culture of the business establishment is such
that businessmen as a group re-enforce nonprofit-oriented behavior, as was and perhaps may still be the case in France, the
entire population pays for this in the form of a stagnant economy.
Alternatively, in Russia, where they are rediscovering the validity
of profit, rent, and interest, the economy is directed more toward
satisfying state aims than human needs or desires. It is also
grossly inefficient. The Japanese, at least until recently, found a
way of combining security with somewhat utilitarian calculations.
There are costs to this also, although perhaps they are not excessive as long as Japanese labor remains cheaper than is labor in
most developed countries. Yet there are obvious costs throughout
the social system that result from utilitarian calculations, even in
business affairs. Some of these, which affect the self-respect of
human beings, are discussed in Chapter 3, and some tentative
solutions are suggested that do not directly affect the capability
of business to proceed on a mostly utilitarian basis and that do
not greatly reduce the incentives for high productivity.

If every social system requires some degree of hypocrisy to
smooth over its rougher spots (an argument we will not develop
here but only assert), better social systems permit character and
integrity. What would we think of a teacher who flunked a
student, not because he did poor work, but because he was a disruptive influence in the school? Who would want to live in a
society, if there were alternatives, where such behavior might
seem or might even become desirable? Yet character and integrity are rule-oriented characteristics.

Many of the claims for opting out have to do with the asserted character of the domestic system or of the international system. If the domestic system is really sufficiently bad, then one must opt out. There is no doubt in my mind that the best Germans properly did this during the Nazi period. (I discuss this topic later in the book.) There are some procedural standards that must be applied before such a judgment is made; a valid criticism of many decisions to opt out is that they are made ahistorically and that, as a consequence, the judgments concerning the state of affairs lack reasoned validity.

Incrementalism also can run wild. A person can become deracinated by justifying particular decisions in terms of the momentary alternatives. In these cases, the individual loses all sight of where one of the larger social or political systems is going and of what it is doing to society and to men. In this case, the individual becomes obsessive; he lacks ego control over his decisions and loses contact with the mainsprings of his personality. He lacks perspective, although in a way different from that of the psychopathic extreme. He fails to be able to distinguish between the immediate result and the direction of the system; he fails to be able to distinguish between the micro result in the particular case and the macro effect upon the system.

On the other hand, the ahistoric person who opts out and who blames everything on a system that in comparison with others performs not too badly may fail to distinguish which elements of the system he is talking about. He may fail to recognize that he is attacking the system in terms of values that are supported by it; he may fail to understand that some elements of the system probably sustain and promote these values.

Can it be capitalism, for instance, that produces racial prejudice? Almost every society and economic system known to man has operated within a framework of racial or caste prejudice. In order to optimize profits, capitalism ideally operates upon standards of efficiency and performance—standards inconsistent with prejudice because they are independent of race, color, religion, nationality, or sex. Is it not likely that the operation of prejudice within the American social system is responsive to some elements of the social structure other than the form of economic organization? What is the system that produces the ghettos? Is it the value structure of the society at large? Are specifically middle-class values at fault? If so, which values? Is it perhaps possible that the failure of at least some middle-class values to penetrate to the ghettos—values of efficiency and performance—prevents many of the residents of the ghettos from escaping? Is it possible that the values produced by the ghetto system perpetuate the failures of ghetto residents? (I am, of course, not arguing for the absurd proposition that aesthetic values ought to be homogenized or that all nonaesthetic values in the ghetto are worse than middle-class values.) If so, one does not want to break up the larger system and opt out of it; one wants instead to integrate the ghettos into the larger system while transforming some specific values and system elements of the larger system that may be inconsistent with such integration.

Ghetto values are in part at least imposed on the ghetto by the larger society. The Jewish ghettos in Europe reflected in large part the occupations the Jews were permitted to follow, the behavior required to succeed in those occupations, and the ways that were required to avoid penalties from the larger community. Many of those values were perverse and destructive, except in the sense of secondary gains. The system in the concentration camps was worse. The glorification of such values is pathetic. The black power movement represents an effort to change ghetto values and to build self-respect. Unfortunately, it is in large part a reaction-formation against destructive ghetto values and, in its very denial of these values, affirms them. That is understandable, if not desirable. It is more difficult to understand the affirmation of destructive ghetto values by white liberal sentimentalists, who thereby accept such perverse values as good for ghetto residents. Instead of understanding that the reaffirmation of destructive ghetto values by blacks is a cry of despair, they heartlessly urge our ghetto citizens to continue to accept their outrageous fate.

Let us turn for a moment to the case of those liberal sentimentalists who want to opt out of the so-called war system. Professor George Wald of Harvard says that he wants to work for life and not for death, for peace and not for war. It would be nice if choices were so simple. Were the Oxford students who said they would not fight for king or country opting for peace rather than war? Or were they among the influences that helped produce World War II? Would the Russians have invaded Czechoslovakia in 1968 if they had thought the Czechoslovaks would fight the way many think the Yugoslavs or the Rumanians would fight? I do not know the answer to this question, but it is at least worth asking. Will the refusal of more and more collegiate Americans to support the American system lead to more and more Russians refusing to support the Russian system? Or is it possible that a dangerous asymmetry in the international system will be created that might drive us into a fortress America and that might produce profound and dangerous political changes within the American system—changes neither desired nor anticipated by many who call for change?

Is it really so immoral to calculate about nuclear war? Only such calculations revealed the basic instability of the first phase of the nuclear arms race and permitted us to move toward a more stable second phase. Unfortunately, technology has not halted and we are moving toward another stage that might be unstable. Yet, only calculations—and even new weapons systems —of the kind Dr. Wald objects to may permit us to minimize these instabilities. There is, of course, no guarantee that the United States and the Soviet Union can coordinate a course of action that will minimize the instability of the nuclear arms race, but it is hard to believe that the United States, acting unilaterally and failing to make the appropriate calculations, is likely to stumble on a course of action that does so.

The international system is not a solidary system. It is possible to calculate in this system in a way that would be inappropriate within the family. There are costs to this process, but it seems likely that the costs are less than the costs of noncalculation. Dangerous asymmetries are not unlikely to arise if appropriate calculations are not made. And Americans may not be the only ones who pay the price if these calculations are not made. Moreover, it is important to understand that these calculations do not determine political policy. They are often restricted to technological components of the situation; they constrain but they do not determine choices by chief executives. They are important influences on the decision but not necessarily the most or the only important influences.

If the president loses sight of the kind of world he wants to produce and of the risks he ought to take to produce that kind of world, then he may get caught up in a process of small individual decisions. He may manifest an obsessive extreme that leads us to a deracinated and mad world. Yet it is very unlikely that the Professor Walds of this world, who want to work for peace in general and who have no hesitancy in making large proclamations on the basis of small knowledge and little analysis, are likely to provide better guides for behavior.

It is fair to point out that spending money on weapons entails at least immediate opportunity costs, that some constructive possibilities are forgone, at least at the moment. But weapons do not by themselves produce war; on the contrary, the appropriate selection of weaponry may forestall war. Sufficient thought about the fighting of nuclear war—one surely prefers speculative thought to a single illuminating experience—may forestall the need to fight a war and to forgo the many constructive opportunities that modern wars foreclose. One does not desire to push analogies too far, for whatever has been true in the past will almost surely be wrong on some occasion in the future. Yet it is fair to point out to those who argue that armaments make for war that the failure of the Baldwin cabinet in Great Britain in the 1930's to produce weapons played an important role in the onset of World War II.

Romanticism, however, is guilty of much more than political stupidity. Although we will not dwell upon this, romanticism has found outlets in most modern fascist movements. If one examines the writings of members of the Black Dragon Society in Japan, of the leftist cadres of the Falange in Spain, of many of the followers of Mussolini in Italy, of the radical members of the Nazi party in Germany, and of others too numerous to mention, one finds emotional and anti-intellectual attacks upon capitalism, the spirit of trading, the process of calculation, and in general upon bourgeois society. Although many of the features of these movements are dissimilar, there is a striking similarity in their attacks upon the corruption, the decadence, the hypocrisy, and the sterility of the bourgeois capitalistic order. The same themes can be found in the writings of the new left in the United States, in Japan, and in Western Europe.[3] The intellectual grounding for such themes, if such a characterization as intellectual is applicable, can be found in such books as Werner Sombart's *Quintessence of Capitalism* and in the writings of the Italian philosopher Giovanni Gentili. Their polar opposite can be found in the bureaucracy, the false intellectuality, the puritanical consciences, and the long, boring speeches in the Russian-led Communist movements. Yet the ease with which individuals have shifted from one of these extremes to the other—Mussolini and the majority of the leading European fascists either started as left-wing socialists or as Communists—indicates that each extreme represents a reaction-formation against the other. The ease with which such movements can shift from pacifism to individual violence to state-imposed violence also seems to indicate the extent to which extreme positions are reaction-formations that suppress the polar opposite in some circumstances and that permit rapid transition to it in others. Anomic individuals such as Adolf Eichmann can operate efficiently within either type of system. They are act-oriented rather than rule-oriented obsessives and function efficiently under the framework of firm directives.

Such extremes are usually indicative of pathological information-processing mechanisms.[4] Although some social and political situations may justify revolutionary activities that "well-adjusted" individuals would fail to recognize, it would be a mistake to underrate the effects of system-induced pathologies on the perceptions, reasonings, and retreats from reasoning of those forced into extreme social roles.

As a neo-Aristotelian, I am a believer, not in mere life, but in the good life. Some situations are so horrible that decent men can only opt out. Yet in other situations, the horrors of the situation can be relieved or eliminated only by appropriate calculations. Extreme decisions with respect to these polarities do little to clarify the situation or to increase man's control of his fate. Both sentiment without control and control without sentiment—both warmth without calculation and calculation without warmth—are monstrous. They are perversions of the human state. However kindly intentioned the advocate, they are destructive of the essential spirit and of the moral nature of man. The man who gives himself up to his feelings and the man who loses touch with his feelings are both men who have lost their freedom, who have lost control of their fate.

Notes

1.   Edward C. Banfield and L. F. Banfield, *The Moral Basis of a Backward Society* (New York: Free Press, 1958).

2.   The possible permutations of positions are more complicated than our discussion states. For instance, one may (a) decide not to calculate at all and to act only on the basis of immediate feelings or conscience; (b) agree to calculate the desirability of a moral or prudential rule but not to calculate its applications; (c) accept some rules without calculation but calculate the consequences of particular applications; (d) calculate about both the rule and the application; (e) accept some rules and their applications without calculation. Each position has a defensible range of application that depends upon circumstances. One or more of these positions may be more appropriate within the framework of philosophical analysis than that of existential action. See Morton A. Kaplan, *Macropolitics: Essays on the Philosophy and Science of Politics* (Chicago: Aldine, 1969), pp. 185 ff., for an adumbration of this position. Inappropriate mixes may have severe consequences for the human psyche.

3.   Dissidence in the Soviet bloc seems much more rational and humanistic. This is a signal irony.

4.   See Kaplan, "The Mechanisms of Regulation," *Macropolitics*, pp. 137 ff., for a discussion of such mechanisms at the level of the social system rather than at the level of individual psychology.

2 Obligation, Education, and Dissent

Whence comes the obligation of the citizen to the state? Is there a style of education that fits the citizen for citizenship? Can education reconcile loyalty with dissent? These are obviously central problems for political philosophy. The problem of loyalty and dissent will recur throughout this book.

From a human standpoint, the state is merely an instrument that can be used for good or for evil ends. Some states function better than others in producing good. Some are more fortunate than others in terms of physical location and material resources. That material resources, however, do not constitute a necessary condition for prosperity is evidenced by Switzerland, Japan, and Israel. Membership in political organizations is determined either by accidents such as birth or by choice and acceptance. For most humans, however, the irrational accident of birth is determinative of nationality and the obligations attendant thereto.

Humans are physically mobile and can move from organization to organization as their means permit; many have done so throughout history. The doctrine of implied consent to a given constitutional order is a legal fiction. Of course, one can assume as a fundamental norm the constitutional order and enforce it within an existing governmental process. But the implied consent of the individual that establishes his willing participation in the legal structure of the society cannot be a matter of positive law. Nor can the normative theory on the basis of which others might argue his obligations under a given constitutional structure be a matter of positive law.

Either the obligation of the individual to a state is a moral obligation—a moral obligation that underlies the entire web of institutional, legal, and cultural organizations—or it is non-existent. Such a moral obligation to a particular state is dependent upon the capability of that instrument for producing good and upon its utilization for good purposes.

The State as a Foundation for Moral Order

Were we to call the state *merely* an instrument, we would misstate the case. We tend to think of instruments as things that can easily be disposed of, that are not essential or of intrinsic value. Food is instrumental to life; yet, although we may dispense with particular morsels or varieties of food, we absolutely require it for life. While any particular form of social or political organization is dispensable, it is nonetheless true that we require political and social organization as a foundation for the good life, for a moral order in life.

But the maintenance of political and social organizations of any kind necessarily involves the subordination to some degree of the individual good to the common good. And this justifies impositions on particular individuals that they would not impose on themselves even if they are altruistic. For instance, the amount of pollution an individual automobile throws into the atmosphere is so tiny that it would be foolish for any individual on his own initiative to cease driving for the good of the community. On the other hand, much could be said for community regulations that restrict the amount of driving individuals do and the conditions under which they do it. Self-taxing measures to support the activities of the federal, state, and local governments would be foolish, for the amount most individuals could contribute toward the collective need would be insignificant. Yet taxes directed at individuals collectively manage to satisfy many of these needs and usually succeed in doing so only by obtaining the greatest revenues from those in the lower brackets, who are the most numerous and who therefore are capable of the greatest collective contributions.

There are other collective prescriptions that are enforced, not by the legal system, but by morality. When, for instance,

the city of New York during the water shortage called upon its
citizens to refrain from using water for certain purposes, the
regulation was not enforceable, for the most part, except by individual compliance. Yet individuals use so little water in
comparison with the collective need that even on an altruistic
utilitarian basis it would have been foolish for individuals to
comply with this kind of unenforceable regulation. It was only
because a large proportion of the citizenry felt a moral and not
merely a utilitarian obligation to comply with such regulations
that the request was relatively successful. In national elections,
one vote weighs very little in the outcome. It can hardly be
worth the effort of most citizens to go to the polls except insofar
as they feel moral because they are fulfilling their public responsibilities. Moral commandments that cannot be justified by individual utilitarian calculations are necessary for obtaining many
political and social goods.[1]

We denigrate the state or treat it in a purely instrumental
fashion only at the expense of the good that it can produce.
Although the state *is* an instrument and although it requires
justification on the basis of the balance of good and harm it produces, we can emphasize this characteristic only at the expense
of the capability of the instrument to function properly. We
are thus caught in a dilemma, and this dilemma lies at the root
of the problem of political obligation.

The Socratic Metaphor

The dilemma of political obligation is nowhere expressed more
poignantly than in the Platonic dialogues the *Crito* and the
Apology. The Platonic Socrates is accused by the Assembly of
teaching youths in a subversive fashion. The Assembly intends,
however, only to impose a modest fine upon Socrates. Socrates
nonetheless taunts the Assembly and forces it into a decision to
execute him. But even this decision is not meant to be carried
out, for it was customary in Athens at the time of Socrates for
those condemned to death to be helped by their friends to escape
to another city. However, Socrates, who had been convicted of

subversion of the Athenian state and of its gods, refuses to escape and therefore accepts the penalty of death.

Whatever the actual historical circumstances might have been, one credible interpretation of the two Platonic dialogues is that they constitute in part at least a moral lesson. As a philosopher who taught only selected students to think for themselves and to question the ultimate foundations of the world, of human existence, and of the state, Socrates was subversive; his teachings revealed that the particular gods of the state were false. Thus there was a sense in which Socrates was guilty as charged. According to this interpretation, if Socrates had accepted and paid a small fine, he might have appeared a mere sophist in the eyes of his students, a man who did not take philosophy seriously and who was merely interested in his own comfort and convenience. Therefore, although he was not subversive in the sense that the demagogues of the Assembly feared—in the sense of actively attempting to undermine the political order—he had to escalate what was intended as a warning, a caution for the future, into a radical and fatal confrontation with the demagogues, the participatory democrats of the classic age. His death also was necessary, for had he escaped, he would have underlined his disobedience of the state, would have appeared guilty of the charges against him, and would have helped to undermine the authority of the state. Instead of educating the sophisticated young to work for a better state, he would have helped to teach the general public disrespect for the institution of the state. Yet his death is ironic, for a truly subversive person would not have accepted the writ of the state. At the same time that Socrates emphasized his loyalty, he also emphasized his subversive lesson.

There is something deeply shocking in the death of Socrates, a death that contrasts so strongly with the request for amnesty of our present-day student rebels. Yet Socrates understood that truth can lead to false inferences if it is misperceived. He understood that those who speak and act have an obligation to consider the consequences of their speech and of their actions: that truth and good purposes are not their own justification and that opposition must be tempered by a concern for consequences. Respect for political institutions is essential to the good life.

Education and Civic Capacity

Throughout human history diverse means have been employed to assure the loyalty of individual members to political or social organizations. Acculturation is one technique by means of which an individual is made a member of the community and of the polity. Symbols are important in this process. Flags, ikons, particular formulations of words, religious sacraments, and public speeches and ceremonies help to bind the individual to a community and to the polity that represents it. These ceremonial forms and claims, although symbolically important, cannot withstand philosophical analysis. The knowledge that one has an obligation to the state despite such ceremony rather than because of it is the culmination of a long and difficult process of training rather than a "truth" that can be imparted at the earliest stages of learning and of intellection.

Child psychologists point out that explanations concerning the natural world that are satisfactory to adults are not satisfactory to young children and will not help young children to find their way in the world, to learn, and to mature. It is a peculiar mistake of our post-modern society that we believe that children and young people are capable of absorbing complicated truths about the social and political world at early ages. We attempt a degree of sophistication that they are not ready for and that is often destructive of their future capacity to govern themselves.

If our goal in our democratic age is, as I believe it ought to be, to produce autonomous human beings, then we also have an obligation to train young people in ways not inconsistent with such a result. Unfortunately, under current social conditions not all individuals will reach this stage of enlightenment; some qualities of intellect, of mind, and of emotion that are not optimal for the fully enlightened are nonetheless socially and politically useful, although with severe costs, in others. Although thoughtful, critical patriotism is better than unthinking patriotism, nations sometimes need their unthinking patriots to offset equally unthinking critics.

No institution except the home is more important than the educational institution for the political socialization of young people. Only part of the function of the school system is educational in an academic sense; another important function of the school is that of citizenship preparation. Although different, the two functions have some similarities, for academic education also is a process that requires certain preconditions, including appropriate attitudes and dispositions, for its successful accomplishment.

The public school system is not and should not be a bastion of academic freedom; the personnel engaged in the teaching process are not true professionals. Flag salutes, the singing of the national anthem, participation in ceremonies building patterns of support, and so forth, are among the appropriate activities of a public school system. The critical activities of the mind should be fostered in areas of intellectual activity where the standards are clearer than they are in the political arena and where instructors are better equipped to make appropriate distinctions. The younger the age of the student, the more destructive can be either ill-informed arguments in favor of the status quo or equally ill-informed arguments against it. The younger the student the less equipped he is to make the appropriate distinctions and the more meager is the historical experience he has that can serve as a framework for comparison. Even apart from the inadequacies of public school teachers, the inadequacies of young minds in handling difficult political subjects militate against their early introduction. The poor quality of the texts available for high schools, the blind and unthinking prejudices, either of the political left or right, to which the authors so often subscribe, present fair warning of the dangers involved in the intellectual discussion in public schools of complicated matters of politics as contrasted with the utility of the cultivation of an appropriate emotional frame of reference by symbolic activities and participation in civic activities.

If the aim is to produce autonomous citizens, the intellectual activities of the young cannot be overloaded at too early a state of development. On the other hand, habits of civility, of intellectual curiosity, of creativity, and of the questioning of received opinions can be instilled at a quite early age. These habits of mind can then be transferred to social areas gradually as the student acquires information and as his mind develops sufficiently for the tolerance of ambiguity, for the recognition that all institutions are necessarily inadequate, and for the understanding that all schemes of reform or of change entail costs as well as benefits.

Failures of the School System

It is a sad commentary on our present school system that it not only produces half-educated and ignorant citizens but also that it produces citizens a majority of whom do not understand or approve of procedural due process and the various freedoms that are requisites in a democratic polity. Much of the discord in our present society stems from clashes between those who blindly support existing authority and those who attack it in a frenzy. In neither group do we find a proper respect for the institutional procedures that support and are indeed the prerequisites for substantive liberties and the good life.

Although it would be a travesty to argue that the turmoil that exists in the nation today is the product of our educational system either exclusively or primarily, it would be just as false to deny the role of the school system in helping to produce poor citizens. The task of producing a citizen body supportive of the institutions, both substantive and procedural, appropriate to a regime of democratic liberty and informed enough to support the political system through temperate criticism is extremely difficult. Yet the task is essential. It is necessary to foster and to sustain attitudes supportive of the nation's institutions and values while encouraging the critical, creative, and truth-seeking characteristics of mind so important to an informed citizenry.

The tragedy of the American mass educational system is

that its benefits outweigh its costs by so little. Although it provides an opportunity for many who would not otherwise have had much opportunity to develop skills and knowledge, the system, with some glorious exceptions, beats many students into either submission or blind rebellion; it destroys their curiosity; it undermines their tolerance for ambiguity; and it turns minds that are potentially fine, intelligent instruments into blunt, crude, and stupid machines.

The reasons for this state of affairs are complex, but at least some of the causes can be adumbrated. A turgid educational bureaucracy, in combination with unions, has managed to frustrate most efforts to educate children adequately. The dead hand of a seniority system, combined with stilted sets of formal requirements, helps to stifle the efforts of the small minority of able, intelligent, and dedicated teachers who remain within the system. Over time, those who remain in the system suffer deterioration.

Beyond this, however, we are faced with the terrible problem that there are simply not enough adequate people available to staff the public schools of the nation. In an age when there are not enough intelligent people to staff colleges and universities, business, state, local, and federal governments, and so on, the teaching profession is saddled with an accumulation of misfits, of vindictive and insecure people, and of people of only moderate intelligence. The frustrations attendant upon the teaching occupation would try the patience of intelligent, cheerful, supportive individuals. The inability of most teachers to cope either with slow students or with brilliant students, their inability to tolerate creativity or ambiguity, their insensitivity to and their fear of the emotional problems of childhood, combine to turn the school almost into a form of penal establishment where rewards are offered for repeating the opinions of teacher, for learning how to observe the world in a stereotyped fashion, and for following the rules. Many who do not conform are punished until they either conform or turn into troublemakers or rebels. The crippling of intellect, of life style, and of emotional expression that the system produces must be accounted one of the tragedies of the modern age.

Improving the system, however, will not be easy. Although the motivations for school decentralization deserve sympathy, plans for the decentralization of school systems and for community control probably will only increase the evils or change them for other evils. Local control will likely interfere with the acculturation of students within the larger community, will likely re-enforce the local prejudices that characterize communities, and will likely in many cases lead to the deterioration of whatever intellectual standards are retained within the system. Under such decentralization plans, the schools likely will become weapons in community power struggles, and educational policy likely will come under the direction of the most radical or reactionary activists within the community. The life of reason likely will be denigrated and students propagandized to accept whatever social or political propositions the local activists desire to propagate. Instead of being trained to develop individual autonomy, the students likely will be crippled and made political pawns. Bad as the present schools are, they are probably better than this alternative or better than Paul Goodman's proposals for eliminating schools.

A Speculative Solution

However infeasible it may appear politically, no solution is easy to foresee that does not do away with the teachers and with the educational bureaucracy. The human manpower is not available to educate young people in a way that protects their creativity, intellectual growth, and capacity for making decisions autonomously. Adequate education probably awaits a revolution in teaching instruments, in teaching machines, and in television programs.

If the nation were divided into nine school districts, these districts could competitively develop different machine programs and different television programs. Great teachers could be paid $100,000 to develop particular courses and even given residuals to make the eventual payoffs higher. The price would be cheap in terms of the potential results and the tax base of the districts would be substantially broad enough to support the program with ease. Such an educational system would probably be cheaper than the present system.

Instead of teachers, these schools would have mostly warm-hearted proctors. In each school there would be a small number of selected teachers, paid very high salaries, who would teach very advanced students, very slow students, and all students with respect to problems of creativity. Such teachers would go over the programs in the teaching machines with their students and show them how to raise questions about the programs and the answers provided in the programs. There would be instruction in foreign languages and questions raised about the nature of words, of meanings, and of applications to the real world. The students would be trained in elementary Socratic methods. They would become young sceptics, but their scepticism would not be directly turned toward aspects of their own social and political system that they were not yet prepared to understand in any depth or detail.

They would be trained in civics, a subject matter that would be designed to inculcate the ideal values of our society and to inculcate habits of conduct consistent with these ideals. They would play-act voting, office holding and other roles in the society. They would also play-act deviant roles or roles of innocent accused, and become acquainted with the protections provided by procedural due process. They would play-act newspaper and radio reporters and become acquainted in this fashion with the role of free speech. They would not be taught that our society lives up to its ideals but neither would they be excessively confronted with accusations of its failure at an age at which they would not be able to receive this information without overreaction of one sort or another. Instead, they would be trained in an open-ended fashion in habits of mind and character that would make them good citizens in the type of society called for by American ideals. They would be trained, in effect, to develop habits of critical loyalty, to be the kind of citizens who will try to make their society a better society for all to live in. They would not be driven by this kind of education, if it is successful, either to a frenzy of despair and rejection or to a denial of the discrepancy between ideals and practices and a defensive acceptance of the practices.

In order to provide depth and detail, courses would be developed in which students would be instructed in different cultures and in different historical ages. The students would learn to work with the raw materials of the particular cultures, to see how people lived and worked, how they fought, how they were governed. An attempt would be made to teach them not merely abstract words in generalized form but also as much of the warp and woof of those cultures as possible. The material would be provided comparatively so that students would be able to use comparisons in making distinctions. In the process, they would be developing historical perspectives concerning political values. The capacity to make distinctions, to use words without reifying them, to understand situations from unexpected and novel perspectives, and to think critically would be developed in these courses, and also in other less socially and politically sensitive courses. Eventually students from such schools would be capable of making genuinely autonomous and individual analyses and judgments concerning political and social questions of contemporary society.

One other function of education must be the inculcation of moral and humanitarian values. Today's big city encourages "hipness"—the view that getting away with something is smart and that only the stupid are honest or helpful. Television, especially but not only the cartoons, encourages the view that life is not real, that the injured are healed and the dead reborn (for instance, the fox and the roadrunner). I do not know how to do it, but children must learn fairness and compassion. They must learn that the injured bleed and hurt and that the dead are finally dead. If our children cannot learn respect for life, for the passions and even for the errors of other people, we are hardly likely to build a world worth living in. Surely the home is essential in this task, but it is obvious that the school system needs to play a role as well.

The culminating stages of the educational process occur not in the grade school system but in the college and university. As distinguished from the grade or public schools, the primary function of the college or university is to be subversive, that is, to pursue truth wherever it may lead. Intelligence is necessarily subversive of any existing order, for it will necessarily expose its weaknesses, its failures, its hypocrisies, and its dishonesties. But such subversion is extremely dangerous if the student is not prepared for it. In a jejune fashion, he then may either reject criticism of society entirely or rebel against society reactively, without perspective concerning alternatives, and without understanding of the damage that might be done to important procedural or substantive rights and interests by well-motivated but ill-advised proposals for change.

I am aware that the university does not always live up to its ideals. Often students are encouraged to accept current versions of truth or trained in minor skills. If it is wrong to accept the sometimes excessive valuation that students place on their intellectual maturity or their capacity (or right) to govern the university, it is at least as bad, if not worse, to help to stupefy them. If it displays lack of respect and a corrupt search for popularity to pander to current student prejudices, it is no better to turn out mindless celebrants of the status quo. Students must be perceived as potential intellectually mature individuals. If they can repeat only what we teach them, what will either we or they do when they leave our sainted halls and we acquire different, and hopefully better, opinions? The proper goal of education is to train students to ask questions they can learn to answer for themselves. If much of student protest is related to a search for counterdogma, students are not always wrong when they suspect the university of failing them.

So sensitive is the political area of education that as dedicated a libertarian as Thomas Jefferson prescribed for his University of Virginia a mandatory textbook in politics, that by the French rationalist Destutt de Tracy. Most moderns would rightly reject this restriction: the essence of the university is the commitment to the life of reason and to the pursuit of truth as seen by the exponent. One important function of the university is to provide an atmosphere within which teachers as scholars can pursue intelligence wherever it leads them. Another is to help students to become liberally educated adults who are capable of self-direction in the conduct of their life and in the formation of their opinions.

The University and Professional Ethics

There is an exceptionally important educative aspect to professional conduct by educators. It is essential that academics behave in a way that re-enforces the student's awareness of the intellectual values of the university. Professors must be honest and they also must be seen to be honest. Duplicity or disrespect for intellectual standards calls into question in the minds of other participants the nature of the institution itself.

Intellectual honesty is not invariably the case. There have been large numbers of full-page advertisements in the press signed by large numbers of professors, in which statements were either clearly wrong or concerned matters that the signers had no competence to speak about. Although the ads state that the academic designations are for identification only, everyone is aware that there would be no point to citing the background of the signers except to provide an aura of authority. Academics should be particularly careful about signing ads and should be especially careful of the accuracy of the statements contained in the advertisements, for careless signing of ads debases academic coinage. The situation has become so bad in some quarters that contending groups of physical scientists privately call each other liars, and there is some reason to believe that all sides are correct. In the recent debate over the installation of ballistic missile defenses around Chicago, a number of scientists at the Argonne National Laboratories made statements that the missiles are continuously armed, a statement that is flatly false.

Apart from problems of dishonesty, scientists often allow

their value preferences to interfere with their critical judgments and then present conclusions as scientific that were determined instead by their prejudices. Thus, for instance, the entire General Advisory Council of the Atomic Energy Commission, with the exception of Edward Teller, initially voted against the project to build a hydrogen bomb. One major reason asserted for the decision was that fusion weapons would make uneconomic use of scarce uranium supplies. The decision was justified in retrospect by the argument that the successful development of a fusion bomb rested on a "discovery" that had not been available at the time of the original decision.

This explanation is unsatisfactory, for it answers the wrong question. No one had asked originally that the existing stockpile of uranium be used to build fusion weapons. The request instead was to investigate the construction of a fusion bomb. It is well known that technological breakthroughs occur in the course of investigation and that one cannot project cost calculations, weapons developments, or many industrial developments merely from current technologies. The Russians developed their fusion bomb on the basis of a "discovery" different from the American. Moreover, uranium turned out not to be scarce. That should not have been unexpected either.

If the GAC had had its way, the United States might have been placed at a severe security disadvantage with possible catastrophic political or even material consequences. Scientists so often allow their policy preconceptions to determine advice offered as objectively scientific that they are extremely dangerous guides to public policy. The antiballistic missile controversy is a recent and compelling example of this.

Professors are sometimes inexcusably careless in their writing. In his book *Atomic Diplomacy: Hiroshima and Potsdam,* Gar Alperovitz, a student of William Appleman Williams, the radical revisionist historian, in his effort to relate the development of the Cold War to a deliberate strategy on the part of the American government, states:

Molotov also renewed an earlier request that the Warsaw government be represented at San Francisco, and he confirmed reports that sixteen Polish underground leaders—some of them political figures—had been arrested on charges of obstructing the Red Army. Although the American and British governments believed the extremely anti-Russian Poles could well have given cause for the Soviet charges, there was little information available, and the arrests seemed aimed at predetermining Polish political issues.[2]

Alperovitz, although he could not easily have been unaware of it, thus ignores the information that the Poles had met the Russians at the request of the American and British governments, after agreement with Moscow, and after a safe-conduct had been given them by the Russians. They then disappeared without trace, and efforts of the American government to learn what had happened to them were frustrated until Molotov's statement. Alperovitz, by emphasizing the irrelevant argument that they might have done what the Russians charged them with, entirely ignored the safe-conduct that had been guaranteed them by the Russian government and the fact that the meeting at which they had been arrested had been arranged by Russia after negotiations with the American and British governments, which therefore had a direct interest in this monumental breach of faith.

Professors and the Ethics of Controversy

It is possible to believe that what one says is true and still to sin ethically in the conduct of controversy. The educator has a particular obligation to foster the spirit of critical inquiry in his charges—an obligation that transcends any fervor he may have for communicating particular "truths" in which he may happen to believe or for impelling his students toward support for particular causes. We have a right to expect an educator to behave in ways that enhance his students' ability to think for themselves. His statements and his conduct ought to manifest respect for evidence and for the ways in which evidence is related to the process of reasoning. There is an even deeper moral basis to this position, for morality involves not merely a choice of values but the process by means of which values are justified or by means of which the implications of particular propositions are reasoned about. A cavalier attitude toward the procedures of justification masks a cavalier attitude toward morality, for the substance of the moral is intimately related to the procedures according to which one arrives at a moral position.

Consider some comments of Chaplain William Sloane Coffin of Yale University:

> Well, there are two types of intellectuals. One is the kind who fulfills the Socratic ideal of a gadfly. He is generally out of power and he insists on asking the basic questions: "To what end? to what purpose?" These are the intellectuals who have been leading the opposition to the war and they are the ones I expect who will go on to the kind of reexamination I mean. The second species of intellectual is sort of modeled after Machiavelli—the mandarin at the service of a prince. That kind of intellectual represents learning at the service of power. It is this kind of intellectual who has been supporting the war and advising the government on its more effective "implementation."[3]

Is Chaplain Coffin really so sure that intellectuals opposed to the war are pure and not seeking power and that those who support the war are in the service of power and devoid of moral values? On what basis is this kind of attribution made? What kinds of evidence does the Chaplain have?

Is it not possible for an intellectual to support the war honestly or to offer the government advice that is either in whole or in part opposed to current policy? Is it impossible for an intellectual to have a private judgment different from the government's public position and yet to feel that it is important to help the government implement its policy as well as possible? Do not critics sometimes oppose the government because their advice is rejected or perhaps not even solicited? Are critics sometimes not corrupted by a desire for popularity, notoriety, or leadership? Is the world so neatly divided, as Chaplain Coffin would seem to assert, into those who advise and those who criticize? Do not many intellectuals change roles frequently or even fill both roles simultaneously either with respect to the same

or different issues? Despite Coffin's seeming qualification, is he
not trying to discredit a large number of intellectuals who have
in common only varying degrees of support for the war in Viet
Nam by an argument that appeals to emotion rather than to
reason? Is he not being self-righteous rather than righteous?

Let us see how Chaplain Coffin treats evidence:

If America really believes in its duty to maintain freedom,
we have to ask ourselves why we weren't crying bloody murder over Trujillo, why we weren't crying bloody murder over
Batista before Castro, why we aren't agonizing over the op-
pression of black men in Rhodesia, South Africa, Mozambique, Angola. A Latin-American diplomat claims that an
American State Department official told him, "in the last
analysis, America will always end up on the side of a dictator,
no matter how dishonest, who is not a Communist—as opposed to a reformer, no matter how honest, who might some-
day turn against us." . . . As of now, Duvalier stays in power
only because of a 20,000-man bodyguard carefully trained
by the United States Marines.

It is true that while Eisenhower was president congratula-
tions were sent to dictator Perez of Venezuela upon his successful putting down of a revolution. Under Kennedy, however, the
revolution led by Betancourt was welcomed. After Trujillo was
slain (some believe with CIA complicity, a practice I would not
defend), the American fleet was used to bring pressure on the
Trujilloites in a way that prevented them from reinstalling themselves in power in the Dominican Republic. It is doubtful that
the Castro revolution would have succeeded in Cuba in the absence of the withdrawal, during Eisenhower's presidency, of
American governmental support from Batista—an apparently
important factor in the collapse of the Cuban army—and unless
government inspectors had turned their eyes in the other direction when arms were being slipped into Cuba. Moreover, Castro
deliberately refused to ask for economic aid that the Eisenhower
administration desired to grant him after he took power in Cuba.
Chaplain Coffin's innuendo implies that Duvalier remains in
power because of American support, but Duvalier has threatened

to seek support from Russia because of American official hostility to his regime.

Why has not the United States intervened more forcefully in Haiti? And why did it not intervene earlier in the Dominican Republic? Although I would not care to argue that American policy is always wise or good, there are some elements of international law involved that make direct intervention normatively costly without the request of the recognized government of the nation. The United States has been quite careful, as it ought to have been, in not directly violating these particular standards of international law, for they do play a significant role in the maintenance of international order. It has supported subversive activities, as in Guatemala in 1954 and Iran in 1953, that involved the covert backing of dissident forces within a nation, but this was done only when the army was ready to support these armed factions. That situation did not exist in the Dominican Republic and it does not exist today in Haiti so far as I know. One can disagree with the government's distinctions but Chaplain Coffin ignores them.

All academics occasionally transgress; they occasionally oversimplify or they occasionally reason dogmatically. This, however, is a tendency to be guarded against. When the major thrust of an academic's behavior is insensitive or even hostile to the spirit of critical inquiry, then his example is subversive of the character of the university. It does not mitigate the dereliction if the particular academic has honestly confused the spirit of critical inquiry with criticism of the government. Such carelessness with factual information, with argumentation, and with the application of moral principles as Chaplain Coffin displays constitutes a kind of moral rape of the student's mind. Even if the chaplain is right as to the moral ends he pursues—and I do not believe he is—his efforts to propagandize students are destructive of the potential autonomy of the student as a reasoning human being and can hardly be justified by the undoubted depth of his feelings. The dereliction is even worse when the individual in question is an academic hero, a man of the cloth, and a martyr to his own beliefs.

Although it is easier to impel people toward action if they believe that they represent truth, goodness, and beauty, and although the government, which is not a purely intellectual institution, must occasionally operate according to lower standards, it is part of the education of young people to understand that sometimes the government must act decisively in a situation that is not factually or morally simple and despite the possibility that it may be wrong not in a minor but in a major way and with extremely serious consequences.

The task of the university, unlike that of the government, however, is not effective action; one important task is to build mature autonomous minds that are capable of critically asking questions and sceptically essaying answers. It is an unfortunate reflection on our times that the government, despite some occasional lapses, has done more to reduce hysteria, to retain an atmosphere of freedom, and to preserve the political process than many of those within the academic community who have attacked it. Part of the trouble in which the university finds itself today can be attributed to the failure of the educational complex and to the poor behavior of academics.

The University and the Polity

The university, as a bastion of intelligence and rationality in the world, must provide an atmosphere within which the members of the academic community can pursue truth as they see it. Thus the university as an institution cannot and should not commit itself to particular political programs of the government or of groups within the nation, except insofar as these proposals affect directly and in a substantial manner its ability to perform its central functions. Thus, for instance, the university should neither support nor oppose the Vietnamese War. Faculty members should be free as individuals to take any position they wish to take on such issues.

To say this, however, is not to say that the university should not cooperate with the government. The university is an institution within the society. It is supported and sustained by the larger society, except when the society is of a character that is inconsistent with the maintenance of university freedoms. The university thus has an obligation to cooperate with government measures, whether at federal, state or local levels, that do not interfere with its central functions. It is at minimum an intellectual confusion, and one suspects something worse, when it is argued that cooperation of the university with draft procedures by sending information to draft boards constitutes university support for the Vietnamese War. It obviously constitutes nothing of the kind. It constitutes a minimal degree of cooperation with the general political and constitutional system of the nation from an institutional, although not from an intellectual, point of view. It involves a working relationship with government—one the universities would be ill-disposed to deny anyway, since they could not survive financially without such a working relationship —that is independent of the particular positions taken by the government, of its involvement or noninvolvement in a Vietnamese War, a mode of cooperation that leaves the professors free to agree or to disagree with the war or even to criticize the entire framework of constitutional order. It is therefore a benign form of relationship—one that is attacked by some professors because of intellectual confusion and by others, and one suspects by a larger number, because of their desire to place the university in opposition to the Vietnamese War.

The relationship between the university and the larger community is necessarily a delicate one. As an intellectually subversive institution, the university necessarily runs the risk of irritating the larger body of the citizenry. Universities are dependent on large-scale public and private support; yet the members of the teaching staffs must write and say and do things that are enormously frustrating, frightening, and mysterious to the mass public that provides support for educational institutions.

The purposes of the polity and of the university, although interrelated, are not identical. The conflicts of interest between them cannot afford to be made too explicit. The universities cannot afford to be politicized. If they are politicized from within, then political control will likely be exercised from without. A corrupt form of power is that of the academic, who, unable to dictate the policy of the government in general, attempts to dictate university policy in opposition to government policy. Although free political institutions and universities can be reenforcing under benign environmental conditions, under most actual circumstances the symbiosis is fragile. The university functions administratively in the real world of politics; the university functions intellectually in the subversive realm of philosophy. It is encumbent upon scholars to recognize the functional diversity of these two aspects of university life.

The autonomous citizen, with rare exceptions, will be a university-trained citizen. As a man of action, he will understand the life of the mind. As an intellectual, he will understand the requirements of action. As a citizen he will be supportive of the state; as a free intelligence he will be subversive. In his pragmatic behavior, he will know how to weave both strands of behavior together.

It is widely accepted, as manifested by the regulations of a number of our leading universities, that classified research is inconsistent with the nature of the university and that research should be publishable and open to access. It is questionable, however, whether classified research is truly inconsistent with the nature of the university. The central professional core of university life is pursuit of the truth. Yet not everything that is true ought to be broadcast. Suppose that a professor of sociology in pursuit of a research project on homosexuals came across homosexuals who had had relationships with the President of the United States. Surely it would be within the competence of the professional judgment of the sociologist to withhold this information to prevent the damage that it might do to the political life of the nation. Suppose a biologist or anthropologist were to develop evidence more convincing than that cited by Jensen that racial groups differed in their average genetic intellectual endowment. Although it would remain true that many members of the so-called inferior group would be superior to many members of the superior group—a factor that would make general group classifications irrational—and that these differences would be irrelevant to political legislation and sociological norms, he might take into account that in a particular climate of opinion this kind of evidence would be misused by ignorant, prejudiced, and irrational political groups. Although the professional would have an obligation not to claim that no differences existed, he might very well feel a moral obligation not to publish his results under these circumstances. We know from biographical and autobiographical accounts—for instance, James Watson's *The Double Helix*—that scientists conceal their results in order to obtain a competitive edge on other scientists in making discoveries. This may have less ethical justification, but it is a normal and not controllable part of the scientific process.

Does the fact that security classification is government-imposed and that the scientist once he accepts the assignment cannot therefore make his own moral judgment about publication make a difference? The scientist does not have to engage in classified research; there is as far as I know no requirement that members of university faculties must engage in classified projects that are carried out on campus. And, if such compulsion exists anywhere, then it is indeed inconsistent with academic freedom. The classified project as such, however, is not inconsistent with academic freedom. The scientist may engage in it because he believes some very important national purpose is involved and that at least for a period of time the results indeed must be classified. Or he may engage in it because he believes that only in this way can scientific information be discovered and eventually published; indeed, much that is published on military matters could not have been known in the absence of access to classified material.

It perhaps may be the case that much, indeed most, classified research should be carried on in institutional complexes that are better suited for such projects than are universities. In many cases, job or contract research is not the most appropriate type of research for the campus. What is objectionable, and what would appear ideologically motivated, is the effort to set up an absolute barrier, to make the distinction one of principle. One suspects that this so-called principle merely masks opposition to a particular war. Scientists did not object to the Manhattan Project, for instance, either during its lifetime or thereafter.

There are deep and important moral problems involved in research and it would be a mistake to minimize these. Perhaps each profession should have a committee on ethics to explore the moral implications of particular types of research. Perhaps there should even be a presumption against classified research on campus. But this presumption, like other presumptions, should be rebuttable; it should not be a matter of absolute principle. The principle is in any event, even in its nonabsolute form, suspect; it fails to permit the distinctions that are really required. It makes claims concerning the openness of research that are not morally or ethically justifiable and confuses the issues central to discussions of this matter.

Despite the growing conservatism of the public at large, universities today are being subjected to a McCarthyism of the left that threatens the essence of the academic institution. Irrational demands are being made upon universities; and techniques such as the use of force and the obstruction of activities of the university are being employed that are inconsistent with the nature of the institution. Many academic administrators, in an effort to maintain peace, are making the same kinds of unfortunate compromises with what are in principle unnegotiable demands that timid administrators once made at the height of McCarthyism. At the same time ideologues on the faculties of the universities either give support to absurd student demands or prevent effective action against disruptive activities.

Universities and Students

There have recently been many demands for student power in university life. Although it is a major function of the university to help students develop their capacity for autonomous self-government and their ability to function effectively as liberally trained citizens, it is also essential to understand that the university is not a political institution and that its professional function is not best served by so-called democratic controls. The argument that students are in a position of tutelage, in many cases well beyond the twenty-first year, overlooks the fact that those students who are of legal age have full rights to participate in the regular electoral processes of the units of government in the United States.

If students were genuinely equipped to direct educational curricula and to judge the adequacy of professors, then their participation as students in academic work would be superfluous. Although it is a mistake to assume that professors and administrators can learn nothing from students (it is therefore a mistake not to have adequate institutional procedures for the expression of student opinion), it is beyond question that students are not the best judges of the validity of what they suggest. Students lack sufficient training in the disciplines and sufficient educational experience to make adequate judgments; they are too involved emotionally during periods of their life when they are particularly subject to feelings of insecurity. Whatever the weaknesses of professors and administrators in determining university standards, there is no reason to believe that these standards would be improved by giving students voting participation in the process. Moreover, such participation would run the serious danger of corrupting both students and professors, with the more insecure or power-hungry of the students attempting to apply their power to young instructors and the less competent or more opportunistic instructors currying popular favor with students. In addition, since most students are not genuinely experienced enough to know what skills they are likely to require as part of a liberal education, giving students too much freedom in curricular requirement choices would run the most serious risk of crippling their later capacity for autonomy.

Moreover, students do not understand the differences between universities. American universities and colleges are pluralistic in their purposes and individual characters. Some are research-oriented and others are teaching-oriented. Some are designed to train intellectual elites and others to serve a mass educational function. Many understand their own functions poorly and stress a quantitative standard of research that is intellectually meaningless and often disruptive of what they might otherwise have been able to accomplish with some degree of skill. Students are often right in their criticisms but also they are more often wrong. There is too great a risk that, given power, they would damage irreparably what has become the world's finest educational system at the graduate level. Although poorly advised on the qualities, styles, and functions of different institutions before they apply, students do have, at least in principle, a great variety of educational systems from among which they can choose those that best meet their individual needs. In their zeal to reform education, they would likely seek to obliterate these differences, the qualities that now make American graduate education great, and the incentives that keep great intellectuals—and often great teachers—in a system that underpays them, if not the great bulk of the profession, enormously.

The social life of students is a matter of a different sort. Perhaps the university should not function in the capacity of foster parent, although, if such a change is made, students should be prepared to bear the costs of it. On the other hand, student self-regulation with respect to social affairs should not be permitted to proceed so far that procedural safeguards are lacking for student minorities or that conduct is permitted in student facilities that would shock or tyrannize a minority contrary to their own values or to those of their parents. Social pressure should not be permitted that would force students to engage in practices that they disapproved of. Some of these problems might be mitigated by insisting upon a diversity of social styles in dormitories, with easy transfers from one living complex to another of more congenial atmosphere and rules.

The demands for departments of black studies in major universities and colleges is deeply troubling, for it both threatens the integrity of educational institutions and is strongly contrary to the interests of the black students making these demands. There are obviously areas of intellectual life where knowledge of the black communities in the United States is of great importance to the educational process. Schools of education, for instance, have an obligation to acquaint their white—much more than their black—students with the cultural backgrounds of individuals who might constitute significant percentages of their future students. Schools of social service administration face a similar need. Departments of history should not in general ignore black aspects of American history, and many of them do not. An argument can be made for a black studies program on the same basis as for a Chinese studies program. However, it is important to recognize that courses in such programs normally are taught by teachers who are trained in recognized disciplines, that is, in political science, sociology, economics, history, and so forth. Moreover, neither the faculty nor the student body is selected according to ethnic, religious, or other inappropriate characteristics.

A black studies program taught by teachers selected by race and one that black students helped to control would be an educational monstrosity. Educators with a sense of their own dignity would be demeaned by participation and most would likely refuse to participate. The proposal for such a program would come more understandably from a white bigot than it comes from black students. One could well imagine the dean of a "Ku Klux Klan" university explaining such a program to foreign reporters: "Our nigras are very happy. A special section of the university is set up for nigras in which they study nigra subjects taught by their own nigra professors. Our white students don't take these courses because they lack the background. When our nigras complete the program, we give them a special nigra degree. Anyone who says we mistreat them is dead wrong. Talk to them yourself and see how happy they are and how well we understand them."

Universities and Trustees

Many serious arguments have been offered against the powers of self-perpetuating boards of trustees of universities. In most major universities, the powers of the board of trustees are effectively hedged by the moral authority of distinguished faculties. The trustees do play a major role in the selection of the president of the university and in certain details of financial management. They sometimes do affect academic policy in the sense of determining which segments of the university will receive the greatest amounts of financial assistance. This is perhaps a matter over which the faculty should have greater control, although it is far from clear that faculty control would operate with greater wisdom than does a relatively independent administration.

In any event, however, it will be difficult to hedge the authority of boards of trustees unless alternate means can be found for raising the funds required to subsidize the activities of the universities. Much of this problem eventually may be met in part either by federal subsidies or by introducing plans that tax the lifetime earnings of students to repay the capital input constituted by education. Whether such solutions would permit the great universities to remain great deserves serious study and is at least open to question. It is doubtful that students are well enough informed about the intellectual worth of the universities to be willing to pay the differential that attendance at one of the great universities demands. Unless the competitive position of universities is to be equalized—and this might destroy excellence at any university and thereby destroy the standard that the great universities set for the rest of the system—the great universities at least will require the efforts of rich businessmen to raise the large sums of money necessary to maintain excellence. Even in these cases, however, the plan referred to for student repayments might permit some desirable broadening of representation on boards of trustees.

1. See Morton A. Kaplan, *Macropolitics: Essays on the Philosophy and Science of Politics* (Chicago: Aldine Publishing Co., 1969), pp. 185-196, for a sketch of the normative argument.
2. Gar Alperovitz, *Atomic Diplomacy: Hiroshima and Potsdam* (New York: Simon and Schuster, 1965), pp. 34, 35.
3. *Playboy* (August 1968), pp. 54, 115.

3 The Tyranny of Principles; Guidelines for the Polity

The Greeks were wont to discuss the question of the optimal size of the polis. Surely that was a serious problem, worthy of profound philosophical discussion. Much of the malaise of the modern world probably stems from the degree to which the size and the complexity of modern political organization have created problems that are beyond the capability of governments, let alone of private citizens, to manage or even to understand. It is idle, however, to hark back to the simplicities of the self-governing polis. Although one cannot exclude the possibility that some remarkably creative political innovator will combine the self-governing features of the polis (which were probably overrated anyway, at least with respect to its practices) with the scale of organization appropriate to modern technological society, the rhetoric of democracy almost surely will continue to misstate profoundly the control of the modern citizen over governmental decisions. Moreover, attempts to increase popular direct control —as opposed to making the government accountable at periodic elections—are likely to make matters even worse with respect to the adequacy of the decision processes in meeting the problems that face modern polities.

The greater the intervention by government in society and in the economy, the greater the opportunities for restrictions on human freedom, individual initiative, and decentralization. Yet modern government obviously cannot restrict itself to police functions. The intervention of the government in the management of the modern economy and in solving other serious problems that face society can no longer be regarded as optional. Some modes of intervention will be preferable to others according to various criteria that may or may not coincide: for instance, economic efficiency, environmental control, or the optimization of self-government by individuals in restricted functional or geographic areas of activity. Many of the suggestions that are made in this book represent the author's desire to increase the area of individual or local self-government and self-regulation.

The impact of mass government and mass society on the individual is often destructive of his dignity. It is ironic that the modern world, which is so productive with respect to the creation of material goods that lengthen life and make it more comfortable and that increase the power of society over nature, at the same time in many ways undermines man's experience of himself as an active agent in the management of his own life and in the management of his community. We will not genuinely understand much of the discontent in modern life, no matter how destructively or corruptly it may manifest itself, unless we perceive it in part at least as a response to a domination of man and of nature by a society over which he has lost control. We will not be able to restore man's dignity and we will not be able to restore his self-image as a free autonomous being unless we can find new and creative outlets for this essential element of his nature.

The best plans that can be proposed to increase human freedom will be costly to some people. Although it is necessary to discuss such costs abstractly, it is essential to understand that they are not merely abstract. They fall on real live human beings. They hurt and occasionally or even often they kill people. Even in such simple things as building large buildings or bridges, it is known that on the average so many people will be killed in the process. This does not imply that one should ignore such costs as a necessary part of progress. On the contrary, constant attention to the costs imposed by any particular projected solution to human problems is necessary, although we also have a duty to consider the costs of maintaining a particular status quo. Judgments with respect to social or political institutions thus always must be made at the margin with respect to the costs they impose on people, the benefits they provide, and the ways in which they enhance the dignity of the individual. To say, however, that the choices are made at the margin does not imply that some institutional complexes are not much better or worse than others. The difference between good and evil—except in the logical polarities of the dictionary—is a difference of degree.

Human beings live in a world that is open to influences not contained in our theoretical models. In evaluating projected solutions of social or political problems, it is important not to contrast the model of a particular solution—a model that overlooks so many of the constraints of the real world—or its projected or generalized aims with the actual working of the system it is offered as a replacement for. Rather it is important to contrast model with model and real life system with real life system. One of the problems with many of the frenetic suggestions for solving the genuine indignities that are thrust upon modern man is that they would do so in ways which can be defended only in terms of highly abstract values that have little or no relationship to any real ongoing institutional processes.

There are genuine evils in the world—evils both domestic and foreign. However, neither the existence of such evils nor the fervor or sincerity of those who would fight them excuse or justify some of the outrages proposed to remove them. Although there are no costless solutions and although any who would act are at least partly corrupted by the requirements of effectiveness, those who will be least constrained in their manipulation of other people are those who contrast the evils of the present with the pristine simplicities of their projected solutions. Those who object to the folding, stapling, or mutilation of man should consider the folding, stapling, or mutilation required in the effort to fit man to abstract dogmas that are unrelated to any institutional designs that can be implemented in a world that obdurately refuses to fit our ideas of it. The rage felt by many dissenters is often based on a primal need for immediate and full (omnipotent) gratification. It is immensely destructive when not satisfied. Its rhetoric of love and its *stimmung* to community demand instant gratification and turn into a rhetoric of hate and exclusion when denied. The cry of "fascist pig" is defended on the ground that it is designed to shock others into awareness, but it represents a felt need that is destructive. It appeals to what John Dewey called the "quest for certainty." Those who follow this path are slaves to their appetites.

Those who would be free must respect the freedom of others. Those who would respect freedom for others must respect the imperfections, the ambiguities, and the uncertainties of a world in which conflict exists and in which perspectives are necessarily different. Justice cannot be absolute. Some problems can be solved, more or less. The "solutions" proposed in this book, however, are primarily perspectives rather than carefully designed solutions to manageable and thoroughly examined problems. They are offered as provocative ideas the discussion of which hopefully will illuminate some of the more serious value problems of our national and international society.

The Ambiguity of Language

Part of the difficulty of discussing politics and the polity lies in the nature of language. Words are usually employed elliptically. They convey useful meaning because we "understand" the limits or parameters of usage. They are creative because they overflow traditional usage but often at the price of ambiguity or failures of discourse. Often they are reified and obstruct discourse. Principles suffer from similar difficulties. It was the reified principle to which Ambrose Beirce, that bitter philosopher of the human condition, referred when he stated that men of principle were fools. The reified principle tyrannizes the infirm of mind by proposing as independent of qualifications that which makes sense only when qualified.

Consider a few words or phrases used in political discourse and in political science. Ask what they mean. Is the political system stable? Even biological life on earth is not stable according to some criteria, for eventually the sun will nova. Should individuals be encouraged to choose for themselves? Do we mean free to choose under the influence of an hallucinatory drug? Under conditions of extremely distorted information? Under hypnotic suggestion? Under the temporary experience of an overpowering emotion, and so forth? Did King Louis XIV of France seek hegemony toward the end of his reign? What do we mean by "seek hegemony"? Suppose that all his feasible alternatives were destabilizing for the international system, as there is considerable reason to believe was the case. How then do we draw the inference that his basic motivation was the search for hegemony? What implications follow from the denial of the assertion of hegemonial motivation? Would he have sought hegemony under other conditions that permitted alternatives not destabilizing to the system?

Consider a few principles. Presidents of the United States ought not to lie to the people. Was Roosevelt genuinely at fault in the 1940 campaign in attesting his hatred for war and in assuring the American public that he would do nothing to lead it toward war? Suppose he had been honest and that this had led to the Nazi conquest of Europe and German acquisition of nuclear weapons under the leadership of an Adolf Hitler who fitted the common stereotype of him? Generals should obey the orders of properly constituted governments. But should they do this if following orders would surely lead to the imposition of a disastrous tyranny upon the entire globe? Or if following orders would lead to destruction of the world? Clearly we do not desire public enunciation of a norm that presidents should lie or that generals should disobey orders. Such norms would likely lead to an enormous mistrust on the part of the public—that is, to a credibility gap—and to the dissolution of civilian control over the armed forces. They could lead to enormous political and military disasters in which, for instance, some generals initiated a nuclear war on their own while others refused to participate.

If the principle that the president should not lie has limits, should not the same limitation apply to academics? Such a question is inappropriate for a number of reasons. In the first place, it confuses institutional roles. The function of a politician is to protect public values in a world in which deceit is occasionally eufunctional. The expectations that apply to this role are tempered by this realization. Few expect politicians to attempt exactitude in expression or promise. Academics are expected to be truthseekers. They are not public office holders and their responsibilities are to different institutional considerations. In the second place, even politicians ought to be reasonably truthful. The example concerning Roosevelt and World War II involves a case in which the putative deceit of the president played a clear, direct, and massive role in the shaping of world politics. Even if Roosevelt's projections concerning the future were intuitive in large part, he knew that he was confronting massive evil and that his agency would have a clear, direct, and massive impact on the outcome. If individual academics or even groups of academics assess their own influence in the same light, they likely suffer from megalomania and surely misunderstand the social and political dynamics of contemporary society. Such academics are hardly fit to train young minds.

We speak of the university as an intellectually subversive institution where the free play of intelligence must be allowed full scope. Yet absolute freedom in intelligence is as meaningless as absolute freedom of any other kind. And only a fool would deny that freedom of research would have to be restricted even within the university, under some situational constraints, in defense of other important values. Consider a discovery that would permit any moderately intelligent person to construct a doomsday machine in his basement with ten cents' worth of materials. Permitting such knowledge to be published to the world could not be justified, for it would ensure the destruction of the world.

Some Reflections on Majority Rule and the First Amendment

There are some who interpret the majority rule principle absolutely. But should the majority be permitted to outlaw majority rule? Should it be permitted to destroy minorities, thus preventing such minorities from becoming majorities in the future?

Should a majority be permitted to destroy the liberties of a minority on the basis of an unreasonable classification?

Bertrand Russell supplied one solution for such a seemingly paradoxical state of affairs by enunciating the theory of types according to which a statement does not apply to itself. Thus the statement that there should be free speech or majority rule would not imply freedom of speech for attacks upon freedom of speech or the legitimacy of majority decisions that would undermine rule by majorities.

Still other useful distinctions can be made. The first amendment to the Constitution of the United States could be interpreted as protecting only speech designed to convince other people by reasoned argument. Thus attempts to enflame emotion could be viewed as not protected by the first amendment. Symbolisms, such as the burning of the flag or of draft cards, could be viewed as outside the protective framework of constitutional guarantees inasmuch as they appeal to emotion and not primarily to mind. The Constitution was written during an age that had recently emerged from the earliest stages of rationalism and it is not unreasonable to argue that rational argument was the type of speech for which protection was desired. Although one need not agree that the free play of reasoned arguments will invariably produce truth, it is not unreasonable to argue that the important values requiring protection are those surrounding reasoned discourse. In any event, a distinction can be made, whether the founders made it or not, between the reasoned kind of speech that is necessary if self-corrective measures are to be taken politically, and which therefore should not be restricted except in extreme circumstances, and the symbolisms which support acculturation of the general population. The effective communication of the latter symbols depends upon a virtual monopoly of the instruments of communication.

Consider a situation in which the opinionated newsmongers of the television networks were forced to justify their selections of newsclips and of comments. Although the newspapers would bellow, perhaps they might be held to standards of reason rather than of notoriety. Many of the worst excrescences of recent

American history have probably been ballooned to a considerable extent by the publicity given them by the news media. Senator Joseph McCarthy, for instance, may have gained much of his effectiveness from the coverage given to him by the media. There are some who believe that many of the radical demonstrations occurring today receive more emphasis from news media coverage than support from the communities they supposedly represent.

It would be educative for the public to observe attempts by the media to defend their coverage or by a future Joe McCarthy to justify his use of evidence. Indeed the chief virtue of such a standard of reasoned discourse would consist of the educative value for the public of observing the application of standards of relevance, of assessment of the evidence, and of reasoned inference. In an age in which so much legitimacy is accorded to irrational appeals and demonstrations, it is perhaps not entirely inappropriate to wish that our institutional structures instead legitimated only reasoned discourse.

There is nothing inherently undemocratic in outlawing totalitarian parties or in forbidding uses of emotion-laden symbolisms that tend to undermine democratic processes. These distinctions, however, do not imply that the outlawry of the Communist Party or the making illegal of emotion-laden use of symbols is necessarily politically wise. What is legitimate in principle may be unwise in practice. To outlaw the Communist Party might merely force it underground or into disguise. The measures and arguments needed to sustain such legislation might create a climate of opinion that would go further and create greater evils than those it would protect against. The courts might be overloaded by casework. The standards of reasoned speech, even if minimal, might be hard to define in a satisfactory manner. Not everything that is permissible in principle ought to be done; and some things that in practice produce evil are in principle good.

If principles are so faulty a tool, does it follow that principles cannot be used to obtain perspectives concerning the polity? This is probably not the case, but principles provide only perspectives. They must be interpreted according to circumstances, and they are rebuttable. If we keep this in mind, principles can be employed to raise appropriate questions about the polity. Much recent—and also much past—discussion has centered on the right of revolution. This discussion, however, needs to be qualified by the recognition that modern states and societies are quite complex entities. And there are some relevant things that can be said about complex entities that affect the discussion of revolution in a vital way.

Yet, even if principles are never unqualified, they do constitute perspectives that determine the quality of a civilization and of a moral order. If the reification of principles risks the absurdities of which Beirce wrote, the treating of them as expendable for momentary gains threatens the fabric of behavior that distinguishes tyrannous societies from those in which justified expectations have some reasonable prospects of satisfaction. If bad principles produce evil societies, the absence of principle is equally calamitous. It is the tension between the need to reinforce the moral basis of political order and the need to be effective in situations that threaten the existence of that order that introduces one (although not the only) inescapable element of hypocrisy in social and political behavior. Institutions are far from perfect and the web of hypocrisy often strikes more deeply and more pervasively than can be justified by any reasonable calculation. Yet the tension between the needs is ineluctible, for they are often independent and thus cannot be maximized simultaneously. If the environment is sufficiently hostile so that the tension between the need to reinforce principle and the need to secure survival of the polity is great, the choice may lie between great evils; if the environment is sufficiently benign, the choice may lie between competing venalities. These often terrible choices can be understood properly only by intelligent and properly educated citizens. The failure to produce a citizen body worthy of participating in good polities either corrupts or alternatively threatens the survival of the polity. If one line of attack upon this problem lies in proper education for citizenship, another lies in social and political reconstruction. Before turning to some suggestions with respect to the latter line of attack, the conditions under which one might opt for revolution or radical restructuring of the polity are first discussed.

Difficulties of Radical Changes in Complex Entities

There are certain features of complex entities that impair the feasibility of radical changes. It is, for instance, a well-known mathematical truth that two independent variables cannot be maximized simultaneously. In building a defense warning network, for instance, if one evaluates the alternative optimal systems, he will discover that improving the assurance of detection increases the prospect of false alarms, and thereby of dangerous but unnecessary military responses. On the other hand, reducing the likelihood of false alarms increases the probability that an attack will fail to be apprehended. Although some air defense systems dominate others in terms of every variable, and therefore are clearly to be preferred, nonetheless in the comparison of optimal systems, improvement in some respects involves costs in others. The more complex the system—and an air warning system is comparatively simple—the greater the ramifications of this principle tend to be.

The more complex the system the more likely it is that major changes will introduce large numbers of unknowns, synergisms, and feedback loops. Minor or piecemeal changes in a system are likely, although not necessarily so, to produce changes that can be accommodated or compensated for. Major changes, however, introduce unknown and potentially quite uncontrollable responses. The process of obtaining negative feedback for revolutionary changes and of making continual corrections, although not completely unworkable, is enormously difficult to manage.

The radical changes that produce system breakdown or gross distortion become manifest in such phenomena as the terror of the French Revolution, the great purges in the Soviet Union, the Cultural Revolution in China, and the great inflation and subsequent political aberrations of Weimar Germany. But even the simpler failures resulting from an inability to maximize two variables simultaneously produce their quotas of absurdities and tragedies, thus illustrating the radical imperfectibility of complex political and social systems.

Early in the history of the U.S.S.R., for instance, its revolutionary leadership was confronted with the conflict between maintaining power in Russia and supporting revolution abroad. Those actions that tended to support the revolutionary base in Russia often had a concomitant tendency to depress the prospect for revolutions abroad. Those actions that tended to improve the prospects for revolution abroad tended to undermine the stability of the revolutionary regime in Russia.

Every institution or subinstitution in a social system, as a consequence of its maintenance needs, develops conflicts with the larger system and with its intended function. Within the same social system different subsystems have conflicts with each other, with the interests of the larger polity, and with the interests of their own members. These may be reducible, or in certain respects reconcilable, but they are nonetheless inherent and inevitable. There will never be, and there cannot be, a social system that will fail to produce absurdities from a particular localized point of view.

Consider particular absurdities. From the standpoint of the prevention of nuclear diffusion, the United States could have prevented the nuclear arms race by telling the Soviet Union that the testing of a single nuclear weapon on Soviet soil would lead to an American air attack upon Soviet nuclear facilities. Such an attack would have been an absurdity in terms of American political values and of its developing system of alliances throughout the world. The failure of the United States and the Soviet Union to reach agreement on the control of nuclear weapons was an absurdity from the standpoint of their potential spread to other nations. However, the Baruch plan would have interfered with Soviet nuclear development while leaving the Soviet Union subject to the vagaries of the American Congress, which might later have failed to implement the proposed agreement. The Soviet counterproposals were clearly unacceptable from the American standpoint because there were no guarantees that the

Soviet Union would remain within the arms control system after American "know-how" was transferred. The present qualitative arms race—in particular, the development of MIRV (Multiple Independent Reentry Vehicles)—is an absurdity that reduces the security of both the United States and the Soviet Union; it is also extremely expensive. Unfortunately, in the absence of a world authority with compelling force, or of a self-enforcing agreement, whether tacit or explicit, or of joint laboratories for the Soviet Union and the United States, it would be equally absurd to forgo qualitative research in the arms area or the installation of such systems. The grading system in school is absurd. It directs students' attention to the acquisition of information required to answer tests rather than to the assimilation of interesting and useful knowledge. However, abolition of the system would involve other absurdities involving the natural sloth of many students and the absence of standards for fellowships and recommendations. American foreign economic aid policy toward Latin America was absurd before the Alliance for Progress because economic aid was offered in the absence of the political and social reforms that would have fostered democratic values and internal stability. Unfortunately the Alliance for Progress was also absurd because the reforms would have to have been carried out by incumbent politicians whose bases of support would have been eroded by the reforms. American farm policy is absurd. Farmers are paid to restrict the acreage under cultivation. The farmers then take out of production the poorest acreages and intensively cultivate the richest land. Then subsidies are offered for the purchase of fertilizer to increase production in the areas that are under cultivation. Unfortunately such absurdities are an integral part of the political bargaining that occurs in a representative democracy under current American conditions. To replace the system by one of dictatorial control would introduce absurdities integral to dictatorial systems.

Moreover, revolutions produce their own absurdities. The French Revolution produced both the terror and Napoleon. If it was not inevitable, neither was it accidental that the 1917 revolution in Russia was produced by that genius of authoritarian organization, Lenin, rather than by the democratic socialist Martov, or by a conspiratorial, anarchistic type similar to Nechaev, or that it was consolidated by the organization man Stalin, rather than by Trotsky. Neither was Trotsky's military suppression of the democratic rebellion by workers and sailors at Kronstadt accidental. As the late Italian Communist Party leader Togliatti pointed out, the terror in Russia was produced by the Soviet system and not merely by Stalin's personality.

Yet the issue of absurdity will not merely go away. If we continue as we are going, there will be twelve billion people in the world in seventy years, over three billion in China alone and nearly six hundred million in the United States. That world will hardly permit even the semihumane values of the present. If we continue as we are, we will choke and poison each other with our waste products. It is one thing to talk about the analytic truth that two independent variables cannot be maximized simultaneously, and another to confront the absurdities, dishonesties, and brutalities of real institutions. An insensitivity to the moral costs of such institutional failures is deplorable. An unwillingness to strive against them and to work for those improvements that are possible can be calamitous. Yet to counterpose the perfection of abstract or ideal institutions to the corruptions of real ones, to counterpose the alleged purity of motivation of untested rebellious youth to that of real decision makers, is to devise grossly misleading comparisons. And the costs to others of acting out such unreal counterposed alternatives might be disastrous both institutionally and in terms of human values. There is no abstract solution to this eternal human dilemma. But just as satisfaction with the evils of existing societies is immoral, so is a refusal to act with due regard for genuine alternatives and with due recognition of one's own limitations. Moral autism is not genuinely directed against the real evils of society but against the discontents of the individual.

The Justification of Goals

If one gives appropriate weight to both considerations—that any complex system will necessarily contain absurdities and that far-reaching changes usually introduce uncontrollable variables—a prudent conservatism would seem to be called for with respect to radical change. There are more ways for systems to operate improperly, inefficiently, and unjustly than there are for them to operate properly, efficiently, and justly. This raises serious ethical and moral problems of justification for those who advocate radical change. Apart from the fact that any social decision will produce some inequities for some people, radical changes, whatever good they accomplish, will do many people, or perhaps an entire generation, some, and possibly major and irreparable, harm. Perhaps so much harm can never be justified. Surely, however, the more doubtful it is that good will actually result, the greater the moral burden assumed by those who press for the change.

Are there then some forms of procedural considerations that we have a right to expect the advocates of revolution will take into account? Even if we grant that the future is always in some sense a leap into the dark, do we not have a right to expect that those who take the leap will try to illuminate the darkness as much as is possible? Historical experience provides one possible form of illumination. We at least know what worked in the past and how it worked, even if our explanations of why it worked may not command the greatest confidence. History can at least teach us how many forms of state and society worse than the present existed in the past, how fragile and uncommon are states and societies relatively as good as the present, how often revolutionary expectations have been frustrated, and how often the situation has been worsened by revolutionary efforts. The revolutionary has an obligation to explain on what kinds of evidence he expects his revolution to do better or on the basis of what evidence, in the light of past history, he claims that the present situation is unbearably bad. He must as a bare minimum attempt to justify the costs he will attempt to impose on others in terms of consequences and not merely in terms of motives, sincerity, or enthusiasm. How many revolutionary claims reveal an ahistoricity, a deep-seated ignorance of history, and a callous and callow disregard for the rights of others? What is presented as a moral claim on the future in many cases represents moral bankruptcy in terms of the procedures of justification.

The problem of the justification of radical change might be made more dramatic by consideration of a contrived example, provided that one remembers that no actual decisions lead to alternative sets of consequences that are as definite and as predictable as those employed in the example. Suppose that an individual can push any of three buttons on a machine. One is clearly marked and it will continue the status quo or something close to it. The other two are unmarked. It is known that one will produce an era of great abundance and happiness and that the other will turn all existing individuals and all their descendents into lepers of a new and very harsh variety that is not subject to control and that eventuates in extremely painful and terminal cancer. If the individual now presses one of the unmarked buttons and universal leprosy is the result, how will he be able to justify his decision to others? Will he be able convincingly to argue, "Think how good things would have been if I had guessed right?" Will he be able to argue, "Well, after all, we really are not much worse off than before?" Will he be able to argue, "The important thing was to act for the right purposes; the trouble with the world was that too many decisions were calculated in terms of prudential considerations that biased the results and that precluded working for a radically better world?" The real world is so complicated, information is so limited, and even the status quo is so uncertain, that the argument for status quo policies or even for policies introducing moderate change will be less completely compelling than in the example. Yet the example at least illuminates some important features of the problem of justification.

Let us consider some good objectives and ask how much we can ask others to sacrifice for them. Some hold with respect to Viet Nam, for instance, that the kinds of terrorism to which the Viet Cong resort should not be permitted to succeed in clamping a totalitarian government on the Vietnamese people. Yet, even if one grants this, there must be some upper limit to the misery that the Vietnamese people ought to be made to suffer or even to the expense that the United States ought to be willing to undergo or to the costs that are accepted in terms of internal American reforms to prevent that result. Genocide is a horrible crime. One assumes that a nation might be willing to run more risk than there are potential victims to prevent the successful carrying out of a policy of killing a culturally distinct people. Yet here also there must be some upper limit as to how much will be sacrificed. A nation is not likely to encompass its own destruction to persevere to this end nor would the United States likely have been willing to obliterate all Germans—including anti-Nazis and the passively innocent along with the fellow travelers and the guilty—in order to prevent genocide by the Nazi regime against the Jews. At some point the price required to prevent the atrocity becomes too high. In the same way, regardless of how unjust social and political systems may be, there is probably some upper limit to the price that can properly be paid or the risks that can properly be run to change a system, even if it is horrible. This constitutes a rule of prudential conservatism that establishes a presumption against revolutionary change. But this presumption, as is true of all presumptions, is rebuttable. And there are measures short of revolutionary change that might have more justification than the status quo.

It is not entirely unimportant when considering problems of justification to remember that the best-reasoned case is not always the best case. I believe that the arguments of Herbert Hoover prior to World War II and those of Robert Taft after the war were considerably superior to those of their opponents—but wrong. Taft and Hoover had more intellectual warrant for asserting their cases, if my judgment is correct, but were nonetheless wrong. There is, however, as far as I know, no evidential warrant for asserting that this is usually the case or for glorifying irrationality. Except where the public record of a statesman provides warrant for the belief that his intuitions tend to be good, at least in a particular area, the audience to which his arguments are directed has no warrant for accepting them if they are inferior or poorly articulated.

Intuitions should also be distinguished from assertions. If one child argues that Nixon's orthodox economic policy will work and another that it will fail, one will be more or less correct. This, however, is no ground for asserting that one had a correct intuition and the other an incorrect intuition. This is to make of intuition something altogether mysterious rather than a preconscious intellectual process that defies full articulation. Einstein could not have had an intuition of relativity theory in the absence of non-Euclidean geometry and the Lorentz equations (although there was nothing to prevent him from "inventing" these also). His preconscious mind processed experience and information to "fit" them to the requirements of a solution. A child is incapable of this with respect to difficult problems except in such an attenuated sense that the process is qualitatively different.

Political intuitions are valueless in the absence of the information and experience that provide their foundations, although some minds may be better than others in some areas in processing this information. In the sciences, the relevant information is contemporary, easily recognized, and rapidly assimilable. Young minds, for varying motivations—for instance, some may seek new formulations to build a reputation and others to prove their elders wrong—are more likely to be responsive to information that invalidates past explanatory schemes. However, even "hard," scientific evidence can be pathologically misperceived, sometimes by a large number of scientists, as in the case of the nonexistent mitogenetic rays that were discovered by Gurwitsch and confirmed by others. In politics, the relevant information is not entirely contemporary, is not easily recognized, and is not rapidly assimilable. This increases the tendency to pathological distortion of the evidence and, because of the increased complexity of the subject matter, to oversimplification. Although the motivations that lead young people to be more responsive to the need for new explanations in the sciences also operate in politics, the likelihood of pathological explanations increases enormously and the difficulty of demonstrating the pathology is greatly increased (in the case of the mitogenetic rays, for instance, independent experimenters believed they had replicated the results for some years). The less experience the person has, the more difficult it is for him to recognize his error, particularly if it is an error that cannot easily be articulated. Thus those with little experience who call for major change have a responsibility to be aware of this difficulty and to attempt to take it into account. Those who argue for continuation of the status quo, however, have a responsibility to take into account the tendency of better established people to accept what worked in the past despite evidence for change.

I do not intend to deny that occasionally only violence forces even democratic societies to recognize and to respond to just grievances. If the use of violence is legitimized, however, its self-serving characteristics and its excesses will destroy the polity as a humane institution. If it is hypocritical to deny the necessity of occasional violence in a democratic polity, it is a necessary hypocrisy. Society needs its martyrs and it may also need to martyrize them. It may be small consolation to know that one has been expended in a good cause; it would be worse to be saved for what thereby develops into a bad cause—the legitimation of private force. In addition, continued resort to violence—particularly by minorities—would probably be destructive of the substantive values sought as well as of more general political values.

Flaws in Incremental Decision Making

Although there is a general presumption against radical change, incremental decision making may also have serious and deep flaws. Incremental decision making has been a major failure in Viet Nam. In their efforts to avoid the extremes of withdrawal, at a time when American commitments were small, or of a major escalation and political reform in South Viet Nam at a time when North Viet Nam might have been deterred, the Kennedy and Johnson administrations committed themselves to a series of small escalations that were virtually certain to draw the United States into an ineffective escalatory cycle. The incremental nature of this decision process was related to the consensual nature of American politics, to the need to reconcile and compromise between extremes, and to the inability to justify to the public major changes in the absence of signs clearly apparent to the public that small changes would not do the job.

Incremental decision making in the area of race relations may possibly fail. As the expectations of blacks continue to rise, and justly so, the performance of the government seems increasingly inadequate. On the other hand, attempts to improve the situation for American blacks are beginning to impinge on the prospects of recently assimilated ethnic groups that are still pulling themselves up by their bootstraps, that are fearful of slipping back, and that are wary of the potential competition from blacks. The attempt to compromise has resulted in a situation in which few politicians have been willing candidly to face the issues. The system of incrementalism has led to a process that blurs distinctions, compromises claims, and attenuates the process of change. Incremental decisions in the area of biological controls and eugenic practices may eventually produce situations even more horrible than the gas chambers of Nazi Germany.

Yet we cannot get rid of the incremental decision process, that is, of representative democracy, in some areas without getting rid of it in most areas. And apart from the price that would be paid in other areas, there is also no guarantee that a dictatorial decision process in the United States would have produced better decisions on Viet Nam or on racial issues. The situation of Jews in Communist countries is a horrible reminder that revolutions often swallow their children and pervert their goals. A totalitarian United States might go the way of South Africa. The fact that the incremental decision process is often ineffective does not establish the validity of a nonincremental decision process for the solution of such problems. Although it is true that incremental decision processes will often fail in such areas, there is little reason to believe that nonincremental decision processes will do better and some reason to believe that they will do worse.

The American system does have one substitute for incremental decision making, provided that substitute is used wisely and effectively: presidential leadership. If the president effectively employs his office for the education and leadership of the nation, he has the possibility in some cases of creating a climate of opinion that would permit him to move with relative rapidity in chosen directions. If the public trusts the good intentions of the president and feels that the president is taking the public into his confidence, then there often will be a considerable body of support for what he proposes. The presidency is the one institution in American life that can appeal to the public over the heads of all other individuals and institutional frameworks, that can provide the public with a sense of national purpose and accomplishment. It is the one institution that the public can come into direct contact with. Had President Johnson on either or both of the issues of Viet Nam and race relations taken the public into his confidence—had he explained the motives of American action, what he hoped to produce, the dangers to be overcome, the injustices involved in not acting as he recommended, the costs to be paid, who would have to pay the costs and why—he might have rallied the public to the support of more radical programs on both issues. He might have stood as a bulwark against the growing incivility that has done so much damage to American life. Although he was less at fault than most of his opponents and enemies with respect to the positive increase of incivility, he nonetheless did not do what he might have done to prevent it.

Is There a Presumption Against Any Change?

If there is a presumption against radical change, it cannot be said that there is a presumption against continual and sometimes major change. When any system is considered in context, there are changes occurring continually at its boundaries that are certain to affect its equilibrium processes. No complex system can remain stable unless it makes internal changes to compensate for external changes. Whatever might have been true of much more primitive systems in much more stable environments, the modern age produces rapid changes in population, in technology, in style of life, and so forth. These necessarily feed back into the political system and require changes that, if not made, must entail larger than necessary costs. Although there may be a number of alternative ways to compensate for these boundary disturbances, the one thing that can be taken for granted in a modern system is that if it is not changing, it is stagnating. If it is not improving the circumstances of the members of the system, then it is almost surely worsening them. Moreover, as material abundance increases, and with it the opportunities for better styles of life for all and not merely for a few, the failure of any social or political system to improve its standards of justice and of equitable treatment cannot be justified.

We are living in an age of very rapid change. Thus the solutions that worked in the past are likely to become obsolete much faster than past experience would otherwise indicate. For this reason we need a much greater receptivity to change and experimentation than past generations required. Military planners frequently put seed money into different design concepts simultaneously. This kind of design concept is required in other areas as well. Attempts to legislate a single solution to the social and political problems that face us will deprive us of a competitive standard in an age in which serial adaptive efforts are likely to prove too slow. The more such efforts can be decentralized, the more likely they are to prove adaptive to different environmental conditions and responsive to adequate feedback. The responsiveness to social and political innovation required by our rapidly changing world will likely prove costly psychologically; it will deprive us of the reassurance that the habitual and the customary provide. For this reason also, a flexible responsiveness to environmental differences and more decentralized decision making are likely to prove essential.

Some Failures of Modern Capitalism and Some Suggestions

Consider for a moment our system of modified capitalism. This system is likely justified in terms of economic productivity, individual initiative, and minimization of government controls. On the other hand, it is a system the costs of which are often thrust upon the individual, who is made to bear not merely the economic price but the psychological and sociological price as well. For instance, the system is overly inflationary at full employment. Under some economic conditions, it is advisable in terms of long-run economic growth to slightly increase the unemployment rate. However rational and justified this may be in terms of the economic system and in terms of the increase of the gross national product, the result is failure for particular individuals. The fact that they are unemployed or underemployed at a time when most others have work is regarded by the individuals themselves and by most other people as personal failure. If men are involved, they usually suffer a severe loss in masculine pride. If their wives are working and supporting the families during the interim, this introduces disturbances into the family relationship.

The dole, unemployment relief, and social welfare may suffice to keep the unemployed alive, but at a considerable price in terms of their psychological and sociological behavior. If the decisions that led to this unemployment were clearly attributable to the actions of particular individuals, perhaps the unemployed would not cognize their unemployment as personal failure. Where a diffuse and anonymous system produces the result, this is not the case. Surely in our now rich system, ways can be found to mitigate these destructive consequences.

There are probably other consequences of our system of modified capitalism that are inherent in it or in modern economies in general and that cannot be entirely changed. The tendency to treat everything in terms of its cash value perhaps can be mitigated but not entirely changed in a system in which the market mechanisms determine price level. Yet the alternative to market mechanisms probably involves a dictatorial decision making process that would decrease the capability of the system to satisfy the desires of individuals. The meaningless quality of the work most people do probably cannot be changed until genuine automation is upon us, and perhaps not even then. The Madison Avenue types who create demands for products that they are dimly aware are valueless, the salesmen who push products they do not genuinely believe in, the assembly-line men who work on a monotonous small part of a larger product, and the laborers who regard their work as a form of degradation seem inescapable in current economic systems, whether capitalistic or socialistic. In socialist economies, assembly-line work goes on and floors need to be swept and garbage hauled; whatever may be said about the valuelessness of consumer products in the United States, clearly most citizens of the socialist countries are eager to obtain such products in preference to the products of their own economies.

Although there is much alienation from work and although hippie tribes and other outlandish groups attest to the development of a nonproductive psychology in the United States in a reaction against our economy of abundance, the very solutions their styles of life seem designed to achieve would be impossible to attain if the bulk of the population were to follow their example. Their survival depends on a continued high level of abundance and of economic productivity in the United States. Hippie types like to talk about how little they require to live. They fail to understand that life in mass urban complexes—and these cannot be avoided in the absence of genocide—would quickly become impossible unless skilled and unskilled people kept the equipment of modern life in operating order and running. The facilities we take for granted—lighting, transportation, repair work, building construction, garbage removal, and innumerable others—rest upon a foundation of at least semiconscientious work. Without this foundation, modern life would run down, our cities would quickly become uninhabitable, and pestilence and death would assume epidemic proportions.

If hippies are a dysfunctional aberration of the system, there is nonetheless a genuine need to compensate for the anonymity of the allocatory mechanisms of the economic market, to introduce greater community solidarity and more style and feeling into life. There is a need to compensate for many of the abstract, universalistic, efficiency-oriented mechanisms of modern life with more diffuse, emotive modes of behavior. We need a growth of community in the United States—not, however, in the form of participatory democracy with its attendant dangers of populism, local prejudice, and tyrannical impositions on local deviants. We need greater involvement of the citizen in his community and in its activities.

Some Failures of Bureaucratic Government and Some Suggestions

Under contemporary conditions, our bureaucracies operate upon an inert citizen body with only limited feedback from them on performance, except in the cases of some regulatory agencies where the interests supposedly controlled by the agencies are overly powerful and influential in their operations. Although these latter cases are not representative of bureaucracy, they do indicate the degeneracies that can develop. The FAC and the airlines, the FCC and the television networks, the FPC and the utility interests, form a network of interlocking perspectives, interlocking interests, and horizontal mobility that often operates against the individual citizen as consumer. The boards of education, the supervisory associations, and the teachers' unions often form a tight network against students and parents. The arresting officers, the parole officers, and the courts often form a network against apprehended youths. Through close association, common interests and common perspectives develop in a manner that turns the entire system into one that is loaded against the person who comes within its toils.

Yet the very factors that make the bureaucracy unresponsive to local needs simultaneously reinforce a number of desirable characteristics. Bureaucratic rules tend to be impersonal. They tend to preserve procedural safeguards. They tend to provide for the representation of diverse and conflicting interests. The individuals who staff the federal bureaucracies usually have diversified backgrounds and diversified reference groups to which they respond. Although many of the same safeguards and procedures are observed in the federal legislative process, the formality and normative neutrality of the bureaucracy re-enforce even more strongly than the legislative process standards of universality, equity, and due process. The great distance of the decision process from the heat of controversy, in combination with the other factors mentioned above, re-enforces desirable aspects of the decision making process.

Although some aspects of desirable bureaucratic procedures can be built into local popular councils, the restricted nature of the locality and of representation, the reduction in diversity of participants, the lack of training of the participants in procedures that safeguard individual rights, and the greater involvement in controversy and greater direct interest in the outcome tend to undermine the ability of local groups to act dispassionately. They are unlikely to preserve individual rights or the rights of particular groups not adequately represented in the process and are likely to re-enforce local populist tendencies toward suspicion, paranoia, and fear of outsiders. Decentralized school control in New York City aptly illustrates these dangers.

One way to compensate for the deficiencies of bureaucracy and avoid the evils of local control is to have local groups assist in the administration of particular programs within the framework of national guidelines. This would produce feedback that indicates where the guidelines are wrong, either in general or for particular areas. If it is recognized that the major function of the local group is not to determine policy but to provide feedback with respect to implementation of the program under local conditions, there can be genuine local participation but within the framework of approved national standards. There should be room for much more local participation of this kind in school systems, in police functions, in welfare activities, and in many sorts of governmental activities that impinge directly on local styles of life. There should be much more opportunity for popular participation in government in this sense, and provisions should be made for much greater responsiveness at city, state, and local levels to information feeding back through such channels.

As desirable as this approach appears to be, there would be many pitfalls and difficulties in implementing it. At worst, however, it is likely to introduce at least minimal improvements into the existing system. If sufficient skill and imagination are invested in implementation, it is likely to make for significant improvements in the relationship of the citizen to his government.

Such an arrangement can be thought of as a surrogate for the view that all or even most decisions should be made democratically. Representative democracy has long been recognized by political philosophers as superior to direct or participatory democracy because of the at least limited checks it places upon demagogic performance. The representative institution, although very far from perfect in this respect, does tend to improve standards of reasoned performance. In large communities it establishes a diversified reference group situation in which cosmopolitan values are re-enforced. Formal procedural processes that in general tend to re-enforce liberties and other substantive rights are enhanced. Although inferior to the courts and also to the bureaucracy, representative institutions are superior to direct democracy in these respects.

Apart from the previous considerations, participatory or direct democracy is not practicable because too many important decisions in our modern complex society are of a technocratic nature, or depend upon a particular type of experience, or depend upon the inflow of or access to specific types of information. Many other decisions must be made within a context or a time span that does not allow for extensive discussion.

Democratic systems function best when officials are accountable to the public rather than when the public controls policy. This accountability is not fully effective and also has many defects. However, it is not necessary that all decision makers be accountable in the usual democratic sense in a democratic system. Civil servants are accountable not to the public but to elected officials who in turn are accountable to the public.

Many of the institutions of the civil society are outside the framework of the political system and are accountable only to restricted subsets of the general population, sometimes to quite restricted subsets. Thus most universities, for instance, are accountable in their own operations to self-perpetuating boards of trustees who in turn are held in check by the pragmatic power of the faculty as exercised either through protest or through the threat of leaving or the actual decision to leave. The autonomy or accountability of such institutions within the general framework of the polity is an indirect one. If they behave too badly, they run the risk of political intervention—an intervention that would likely be destructive of their primary functions.

Although accountability does provide a check upon governmental—and even upon private institutional—performance, even this instrument is of limited value. In an age when technology enhances individualism and self-assertion—although we can hardly exclude the possibility that dehumanization will be the terminus of this process—the problems that face government are so complex and the relationship between action and result so indirect that even specialists have little right to assurance concerning adequacy of performance. It is perhaps for the very reason that the specialists and informed administrators who play such a large role in the decision process are aware of the inadequacies of their information, their theories, and their prescriptions, that government is in general less assured and less confident than the critics who assail it. Knowledge of complexity decreases confidence in one's own answers and in simple answers in general.

The tolerance of ambiguity and uncertainty that is necessary for adaptation to current conditions requires enormous self-discipline. The inability on the part of the public adequately to be able to judge policy reduces the meaningfulness of the concept of accountability. The fact that single elections determine choices when diverse policies are at issue also reduces meaningfulness. Yet, defective as accountability is, there is a judgment day; whether they are rightly or wrongly judged, officials have their fate decided by that verdict. The difficulties of accountability are inherent in the nature of modern society. If we cannot return to what now appear as the pristine simplicities of earlier ages, then perhaps we must learn how to live with the complexities of the present. Perhaps the only meaningful alternative is the kind of local and limited participation discussed earlier.

Although man is a political animal and although the development of his human capacities requires his activity, not merely in the act of voting, but in the governing process, this type of act is best exercised in areas where his direct interest is closely engaged and where his competence is sufficiently great so that the substantive defects of nonprofessional decision making are reduced to a reasonable minimum. Thus, we ideally look forward to a day when local communities, businesses, and educational institutions find appropriate areas for individuals to engage in self-government.

The important operative word is "appropriate"; control of students over curriculum, faculty, or financial policy of a university would be a travesty. This would not be self-government; it would be a form of mob rule. From the educational point of view, it would establish exactly the wrong lesson; it would establish the dominance of the appetites over reason. It would blunt the capacity of students to develop a reasonable form of autonomy by instilling the lesson that experience and expertise are valueless. If all are fully capable of governing from the beginning, then where is the value of becoming liberally educated, except in gaining possession of a piece of parchment?

The idea that politics must proceed in full open view of the public is as misleading as is the notion of full participatory democracy. The Paris peace negotiations on Viet Nam illustrate this lesson. The official meetings are devoted to propaganda that serves public political functions. The real business occurs behind the scenes, safely insulated from the public pressures and considerations that would otherwise vitiate the possibilities for agreement, small though they may be anyway. Although it is not true that no effective deliberations can occur in public, many cannot. Efforts, for instance, to open to public view departmental decision making procedures in universities would merely force the confidential negotiations into a different and more informal and more easily corruptible sphere.

Some Other Citizenship Roles

There are numerous ways in which the individual can contribute to his community and to his nation other than participating in local governing bodies. These involve a more positive orientation on the part of citizens to their government. We hear many complaints about the quality of the police. Perhaps what we need is a national police academy equivalent to West Point or the Naval Academy. If those going to such academies know that they will be assigned to commissioned roles immediately upon graduation, the police forces will provide a clear professional career line for people of substantial merit.

Enlisted positions in the police—or in other worthwhile social activities—might be handled by draftees. If we consider what we gain through citizenship, why should not each individual give his government two years of service in one form or another? Draftees who serve in the police would not have time to acquire the typical prejudices of many police. They would not, in their capacity as policemen, constitute an upwardly mobile group seeking to differentiate itself from the classes from which they or their families have recently removed themselves. They would be more subject to strong leadership from the police officer class. They would not have an opportunity to form associations of their own to lobby for their provincial points of view.

During summers, high school youths could be mobilized for neighborhood cleanups. Social roles could be found for the handicapped; various forms of cultural roles could be sponsored for the idle. Mothers without husbands could be paid to bring up their own children; such a role could be viewed as a socially responsible role rather than a dole. Créches for working class mothers could be built.

College students could receive tuition loans from the government, if they desire, which would be treated as a capital input. They would then pay back the loan through a fiat rate tax (per unit of input) on all future income. Income from this source that exceeded outgo could be used to subsidize those elements of the population who have social backgrounds that deprive them in ways that make attendance in college less likely and who thus are not likely to receive this particular capital input from society. These are just a few suggestions. There are numerous ways in which the walls of isolation that surround our citizens in contemporary society could be broken down and in which our citizens could be made much more active members of their community without the dangers of populism. There are ways in which the stigma can be removed from payments made to worthy individuals in handicapped circumstances. In a society that maintains the value of work and service, payments to handicapped people, particularly if the payments were made for socially useful work, would likely have neither the stigma of a dole nor the psychological consequences of the dole that re-enforce dole-receiving activities. Society should not view such people as receiving a dole nor should their image of themselves be of such a character. And of course, those who are temporarily unemployed could be brought within the framework of the system and assigned tasks to perform in return for wages received.

The Draft and Conscience

Although the risk of life and limb upon entry into the armed forces is quite small, some individuals do enter combat and do run this risk in a direct way. There can be no doubt of the moral anguish a person must feel if asked to serve in a war he considers immoral or even unrelated to any reasonable national security goal. The present draft system is particularly offensive because it excludes (often effectively permanently) middle class college children at a time when the objective of preserving a reservoir of skilled and intelligent people is not a national problem. The draft is thus in effect a form of class (or even partly of race) legislation designed to respond to political pressures from middle class parents. Moreover, the local draft boards are thoroughly corrupt and indecent institutions in which favoritism, prejudice, and local ties play prominent roles. (In some of my army positions during World War II, I gained extensive knowledge of such derelictions.)

Yet the alternatives to the draft appear to me to be even worse. A volunteer army—even if it were possible to raise one—would in effect attract into the service those from lower economic groupings. It would entice those in our society who are poorer to run risks for those of us who are richer (and in general those who are blacker for those who are whiter). Although we do this in ordinary private civil life—those who work on skyscrapers, for instance, get paid for accepting the risks—it seems wrong to utilize the same principle in pursuing collective goals. Moreover, this process dissolves the principle of civic obligation into one of a cash nexus. Surely defense of the nation's interests is an obligation that rests on all of us in principle even if a process of selection (on some reasonable principle) is, or ought to be, employed.

We have established decision making processes in our society for making decisions. Even though our involvement in Viet Nam was in some ways primarily an executive decision, the draft system and the appropriations for the services also require Acts of Congress. We do not permit the principle that individuals will pay taxes only for purposes of which they approve. Those purposes are determined according to constitutional processes. It is true that much more is at stake in the draft. Yet, if we do permit individuals to object to war in general, it does not follow that this privilege ought to extend to particular wars—an evaluation that can be made only in particular circumstances, that is particularly subject to self-serving rationalizations, and that is particularly difficult to judge. Indeed, acceptance of the penalty of law may be the best test of conscientiousness. Although only the hard of heart would desire to force young people into cruel choices, it is also true that conscience does not thrive on easy choices. Combat is not easy either. Moreover, every middle class (and more often white) youth who evades the draft forces another lower class (and more often black) youth into his place. Should this process be eased?

No sensitive person could be unaware that the draft is particularly frustrating when a war is undeclared and when the bulk of society suffers little direct effect or even receives profits from it. Elementary feelings of justice are offended. There may well be limits to our tolerance as a nation for this process and, as a consequence, we may be forced into cruel choices.

On the other hand, the idea of the draft, whatever the difficulties and exigent limits of particular applications, appears sound. The draft is not involuntary servitude. We are Americans by accident of birth. The riches and privileges and the civilized polity that belong to us—and that most others on earth would make enormous sacrifices for—were not earned by us. If we do not wish to help to preserve our institutions, we can choose freely to leave. If we wish to protest the morals or judgment of those who have been elected to decision making positions, we can accept the penalty of law. This is not easy, I know, but it does have dignity and would manifest courage. And, as in the case of the Platonic Socrates, it can constitute a moral lesson. For those who are truly conscientious, this ought not to be entirely without value.

Some Aspects of the Racial Issue

Some discussions of the racial issue in the United States attempt to compare it to the assimilation of other ethnic minorities. Although blacks have been in this country for some four hundred years, so the argument goes, the process of assimilation is just beginning. In the end it will progress as successfully as with other ethnic minorities. This argument, although well-intentioned, overlooks some practical matters. Most other ethnic minorities were able to melt into the general population by the second generation. By adopting appropriate styles of dress, speech, manner, and appearance, the sons of the immigrants were in many cases indistinguishable from the rest of the population. The major exception to this was the Oriental immigrant, who had the compensating advantage of very strong community organization, and who, in any case, was not able to rise very far or very fast in the social hierarchy until the period subsequent to World War II. Even now, Oriental labor is still cheap labor in the United States. The rise of the black community has been impeded in part at least by well-intentioned social legislation.

Minimum wage laws have reduced the capacity of blacks to outcompete whites for jobs, as earlier immigrant groups outcompeted those already here by offering themselves for lower wages. Nonetheless, when all this is taken into consideration, blacks, except for those whose skin color is light enough to pass, are separated from the rest of the population by an external distinguishing characteristic. A black traveling on the Illinois Central Railroad from Chicago to the South will inevitably notice, as do whites, that all conductors (who hold what is not the world's most highly skilled job) are white and that all porters are black. Although this particular type of discrimination probably results more from union monopolies than from employer prejudice, the impact on the psyches of the black travelers must be quite deep.

Discrimination of this type re-enforces an expectation of failure that is widespread within the black community, an expectation that is shared by the white community, and that is transmitted, often subconsciously, in the teaching process, by both black and white teachers. Although the black youngster lacks the advantages of home environment of most white children with respect to the acquisition of intellectual capabilities during his earliest and most formative years, his capabilities are further dulled by the expectations of his own group and those of white groups during the educational process. We are confronted with a vicious cycle of defeat that cannot be overcome without enormous effort. Unless we overcome it, we will do deep damage to the American values of equal opportunity and universalism. It will be a damage that has wide repercussions through the social and economic systems.

On the other hand, many liberals have been paying less attention to constructive proposals than to forms of self-abasement in response to demands by radical blacks. It reveals a very deep sense of prejudice and unwarranted condescension to think that blacks are so inherently different and so childlike they must be permitted standards of behavior that would not be tolerated in whites or that such poses represent the black community. The incivility that has been generated by this has now spread into wider areas and threatens to debase levels of conduct and belief in the United States.

Just recently William Sloane Coffin has argued that the trial of Bobby Seale for murder in New Haven is legally right but morally wrong because the nation is responsible for Seale's state of mind. In addition to further raping the minds of his students by urging them to mindless emoting, the Reverend Coffin has implicitly resurrected in new guise the old Southern racist view that the murder of one black by another need not be punished because blacks are inherently irresponsible and worthless. Arguments similar to those used by the reverend could be used to absolve Southern lynch mobs and Nazi gas chamber murderers. Perhaps we should be grateful to the Reverend Coffin for making clear his moral, or rather immoral, premises.

Much nonsense, both in terms of incivil behavior and in terms of intellectual argument, has been accepted from radical black leaders, who represent the black community, originally at least, by virtue of their notoriety in the American press. It is not true that black communities are a colony within the United States, although radical blacks may eventually turn them into such, or that blacks built this country with slave labor. The examples of India and China demonstrate the value of labor in the absence of capital, technology, and organizational skill. It is noteworthy that the South, which "exploited" black labor more than any other section of the country, is just beginning to emerge from its period of economic underdevelopment.

The rhetoric of exploitation constitutes in general, although not in every particular, the worst kind of intellectual nonsense. Moreover, the attempt to manipulate feelings of guilt will in all likelihood prove counterproductive. There is a limit to how much guilt people can live with and a serious question with respect to the extent to which guilt is intellectually justified in any case. America will not be motivated to do what is right and necessary in the area of race relations—particularly given the fact that much of the burden falls on groups that have recently risen in the social hierarchy and that are in some danger of falling back into the position from which they came—until it can be made clear that the reasons for doing something about the problem are directly related to the nature of American values and ideals, to important consequences for the social and political life of the nation, and to the kind of world we desire to build for our children.

On the other hand, there was a conspiracy, partly implicit but apparently partly explicit, to force blacks into particular neighborhoods at inflated costs. Savings and loan banks and ordinary savings banks apparently participated in this conspiracy by refusing mortgages to blacks, many of whom would have been eligible for mortgages by ordinary standards, in favor of whites who then sold the same houses to blacks on contract at inflated prices. It is up to the courts to dissolve these conspiracies and to assess adequate penalties, some of which it is to be hoped may force changes in the organization and leadership of the offending institutions.

Many radical blacks and a number of radical whites assert that the United States is a racist society. Although it is true that many evil consequences of discrimination are present in our society and that we surely cannot afford to remain contented with what we have done to date, the fact that American society has not suppressed or even attuned itself to strong and coherent demands for suppression of rioting, violence, and extreme verbal statements is a sign that racism runs contrary to the values of our society. This does not mean that there are no dangers; extreme and radical attacks upon the institutions and values of the society by radicals in the name of a fight against racism might possibly release repressive energies that are currently held in check by the ambivalences that characterize most people. Nonetheless the resistance of American society to such a solution is enormous. Black radicals who proudly proclaim that they will not meekly accept the fate that Jews accepted in Germany overlook the fact that were American society at all like that of the Germany of the 1930's, they would already have been brutally repressed. The extreme demands that have found expression in America would never have been permitted to emerge.

We obviously cannot, and we surely ought not to want to,

return to the conditions under which blacks accepted caste inferiority. Unless we solve this problem, we will be forced both by white and by black radicals to move in the direction of the kind of apartheid they have in South Africa. Such a transition would subvert the institutions of this country and do enormous damage to the values Americans have fought for and died for.

The reasons for firm action have nothing to do with the feelings of guilt felt by so many white liberals. Moreover, the rhetoric of black radicals, which demands handouts in the guise of recompense for the past, will merely re-enforce in blacks the feelings of inferiority and helplessness that so many of them now feel. The measures that need to be taken, and which obviously require careful study, must involve much self-help in the black community. Large gifts of the kind demanded by so many radical black groups are politically infeasible and would be immensely destructive to the black community if they could be obtained.

It would be far more useful if self-generated projects originated in the ghettoes that obtained support on their merit, as opposed to demands that either serve as crutches or that represent a form of gangsterism. One such project might involve an effort to train poor mothers (whether black or white) how to facilitate their children's intellectual growth during the crucial first three or four years. Such a project might also do more to resolve long-term needs than tens of billions of dollars spent at the direction of the federal government. It should be fairly easy to get volunteer help from universities for pilot projects and to make a demonstration of such an order that funding would be seen as a compelling necessity and the project itself as a demonstration of the human dignity and worth of those who originated and carried it out.

Although the black bourgeoisie, in its effort to distinguish itself from the black proletariat, has failed to engage in the kinds of civic and cultural activities that would be of general benefit to black people, it is not true that "making it" is the wrong solution for blacks. There is a gulf between the black bourgeoisie and the black proletariat that will be difficult to overcome and that hopefully some black college students are trying to overcome, although in very misguided ways, at the present time. The black proletariat will not rise in social and economic accomplishment overnight. But it will not rise at all unless an educational solution is found for its problems.

A Plea for Community Design

It is extremely important to eliminate the types of welfare programs that are so destructive to pride among poor people generally, whether black or white. In addition, our cities are going to have to be redesigned to provide a more livable environment for everyone, and in particular a much more livable environment than that provided for by the current grotesque projects for the housing of poor people. What the larger community can do, if it is intelligently guided, is to provide a livable environment in which there is sufficient hope to generate self-help on the part of deprived members of the community, whether white or black. It may satisfy our moral feelings to denounce those who fail to help themselves; but it does no practical good, and a great deal of harm instead, if we insist upon conditions that re-enforce the attitudes we deplore.

Our communities have grown topsy turvy, as have the school, the police, and the cultural institutions that service them. Many of our institutional structures fit very poorly together; much more in the way of environmental, sociological, and political design is possible that would vastly improve our ability to live together. Fortunately our country is sufficiently large and diversified so that different experimental solutions can be tried in different areas of the country; nothing will be tried at all unless we are capable of recognizing the problem and of applying techniques of system design to their solution.

Much money is being spent in an effort to overcome these problems. Even more will be spent when the Vietnamese War has ended. Many observers, and the author agrees with them, view most of this money as being wasted and a good deal of it as being counterproductive. It is most likely that we do not have the faintest idea of how to spend large sums of money productively. It would be enormously beneficial if we would take half a dozen moderate-sized cities with minority problems and attempt to find alternative designs for coping with their problems and for re-enforcing the values that would be most coherent with the kind of political and social structure we would like this country to have in the future.

As urgent as these problems are and as intense as are the demands for rapid change, we should not delude ourselves into believing that we possess the kind of knowledge required for a decent effort at a solution to the problems. We are most unlikely to gain time by frantic proliferations of activities that have failed in the past.

If the President of the United States can establish the kind of communications with both blacks and whites that creates an understanding of the urgency of the problem and an awareness that serious efforts are being made to cope with it, it is not unlikely that we can survive the disturbances that will almost inevitably take place until substantial progress has occurred.

4   Loyalty and Dissent

Many of the most critical problems in the relationship of the citizen to the polity involve the connections between domestic and foreign policy, the importance of the state in the maintenance of desirable values, the moral role of dissent, bargaining with competitors, and guarding against manifest and potential military threats. These problems assume greater and greater importance as the world becomes more complexly interrelated.

Although the Credit Anstalt failure is believed by some to have set off the worldwide depression of the 1930's, the growth of the modern corporation into an international giant that is hardly controllable within the national political framework is a post-World War II development. Improved logistics, improved means of transportation, worldwide satellite television broadcasting facilities, ICBM's, and the huge impact of even relatively minor military ventures on domestic programs make it extremely difficult to formulate international policies without considering their domestic consequences.

Although it is not true that the Vietnamese War has led to a cutback in the Great Society—contrast the $25.6 billion expenditures for Great Society measures in 1968 compared with $9.9 billion for 1960 and $12.9 billion for 1963, and the 45 domestic social programs of 1960 with the 435 that were in existence in 1968—much more in the way of social legislation and in support for pure science would be possible in the absence of military expenditures for Viet Nam. It is reliably reported that even so surgically swift an operation as the Soviet occupation of Czechoslovakia has imposed a considerable burden on the Russian domestic economy. Some at least of the pressure to negotiate ballistic missile limitations results from budgetary strains in the Soviet Union and the United States. The impact of Department of Defense expenditures on the American balance of payments and rate of domestic inflation constitute a severe restraint on American policy.

Although much of the argument against military expenditure and military ventures stems from a social science myth about the development of a garrison state, there is no substantial evidence to sustain this thesis. Similar arguments were strongly asserted before World War II. Yet American society emerged from that war as a more just society in which civil liberties were strengthened. There has been on balance no substantial evidence of the erosion of civil liberties during the Vietnamese War; the protection of dissent during a time of military conflict by the courts and by the political administration of the United States has been perhaps unprecedented in American history.

Moreover, it is a mistake to believe that the choice between domestic progress and international security is a direct and simple choice. If the Vietnamese War is either counterproductive to American security or of little consequence to it, then the argument as to what could otherwise be done—but not what surely would be done—with the saved monies makes sense. If, on the other hand, our security would be weakened by a contrary policy, much greater subsequent expenditures might be forced upon us. If we were eventually thrust back into a beleaguered position, there would likely result a diminution in our civil liberties and retrogression in our social progress and in civil rights. Even if the resulting regime were leftist in orientation, the radical blacks who pursue this goal would likely find themselves betrayed as badly as the Jews who supported Communism against Czarist anti-Semitism in Russia. The relationship between external and internal policy is real; it is, however, anything but simple.

Domestic Correlates of International Decisions

At least some of the possible decisions of American statecraft can be fateful for the future of American institutions and also for the maintenance of important values in the world. Let us think back to the forceful debate before World War II in order to explicate this problem. Those who favored aiding the allies talked about the military threat stemming from Nazi hegemony in Europe. Predictions were made about German overlordship in Africa after the conquest of Europe. Military conclusions were drawn from the proximity of Africa to the coast of Brazil.

Conservative isolationists—Herbert Hoover is an example—unlike the liberals who opposed prowar measures, met these arguments directly and successfully refuted them. On the basis of the then known technologies Hoover was able to rebut the argument that the Nazis would constitute a military threat to the United States if they secured hegemony in Europe. Although Hoover did not foresee nuclear weapons and although conceivably the Nazis might have constituted a direct military threat to the United States had they acquired nuclear weapons first, the threat to the United States that could properly have been foreseen at the time—and it was neither a direct military threat nor the danger that we might have been deprived of natural resources—was little discussed in that debate.

The danger the United States faced was neither simple nor easily calculable. The quality of life in the United States would most likely have been irreparably harmed by Nazi victory. Anne Lindbergh was proclaiming a wave of the future, in specific an authoritarian wave. Fascists and protofascist groups were becoming increasingly numerous. To the south of us, fascist and Nazi ideologies were making headway, particularly in Argentina and Bolivia but in other nations of Latin America as well.

A world conquered by the Axis would have been a world hostile to American values. It would have been a world in which our confidence in our own values would have been diminished. The military measures that would have been forced upon us had we been encircled by facist and authoritarian states might have produced major political change in the United States and the garrison state that liberals feared war would bring.

Although it is unlikely that we would have adopted either fascism or Nazism, we would more likely have found our own American mode of response to what would then have been viewed as an inevitable trend of world history. It would also have been argued that only in that manner could we have become strong enough to withstand the pressures arrayed against us.

Yet this latter projection is not something that can be proved. Perhaps the Nazi regime would have mellowed from within. Perhaps its effort to extend control over the continent of Europe would have overloaded it, leading to its collapse.

Perspectives on Moral Questions

Possible Criteria for Choice

How do we make decisions in circumstances so resistant to demonstrated proofs or reasoned judgment? Obviously some of the most important moral problems of our time—and perhaps of history—are raised by the questions related to such decisions. Answers to these questions need to be justified under circumstances of gross uncertainty. Consider just a few of the relevant questions. Was the misery of World War II justified? If resistance to the Nazis led to the deaths directly or indirectly of some forty million people, how do we justify the decision to resist if we assume that this result could have been anticipated by reasonable men? Confronted with the determination of the Nazi regime, would it perhaps have been better for the rest of the world to surrender?

Judgments were necessary; it was necessary for political leaders to act with firmness and swiftness upon those judgments. The men who made the decisions were faced with the moral problem of leaping into the unknown upon the basis of inadequate information—a moral problem that necessarily confronts statesmen when they deal with major problems.

Some of the possible perspectives on those decisions have been offered in the previous chapter. There obviously must have been some upper limit to the costs that would have been acceptable to prevent Nazi victory. Yet perhaps those costs would not properly have been set very low. The Nazis might have established a thousand-year Reich. They might have involved those not eliminated in complicities that debased them.

They might have developed drugs or psychological or biological controls that would have irreversibly changed and debased man. These projections cannot be known scientifically either, although it is important to be aware that the technological techniques that foreshadow them are developing.

Yet there are vast uncertainties. In situations in which little is known and in which radical changes and radical costs are likely to be introduced regardless of what one does, it is perhaps best to follow the advice of Winston Churchill: to do that which is morally right and to resist that which is morally wrong. Although this advice is only a rebuttable perspective and although it will produce historical ironies, it is perhaps the best advice we have.

Resistance to evil is not a simple matter. It produces its own caricatures of the evils fought but it also provides opportunities for heroism and moral courage, for maintaining human self-esteem, and for re-enforcing civilized values that, through millenia of recorded history, have seemed exceedingly fragile.

Much of the debate over current American foreign policy runs aground on intangibles similar to those of the pre-World War II period. Is the danger to the United States that of monolithic Communism? Perhaps division in the Communist world will strengthen rather than weaken its expansive tendencies; perhaps a world dominated by a Soviet bloc and by a number of independent and semi-independent Communist states would be even more hostile to the United States politically and more dangerous militarily than a world in which Communism was unified.

The most crucial area for the United States is that of Western Europe, with its skilled population and great industrial base. Does American involvement in Southeast Asia detract from its ability to form a stable relationship with Europe and to aid in the protection of Europe, or is the credibility of the American guarantee in Asia, if not a prerequisite, an important ingredient in the credibility of American performance in Europe?

Can questions of this kind be answered in the abstract? Or is it a matter of balancing risks, resources, and uncertainties, in which case evaluation is impossible in an absence of the specific relationship of resource to risk to uncertainty, that is, in the absence of a specific analysis of the particular case? Do the answers, in addition, depend upon the historicity of the case, that is, of the specific sequence of events that lead to decision and to the expectations and interpretations that develop in the context of the decision making process? Although rebuttable perspectives can legitimately and usefully be offered that are relatively independent of resources, specific alternatives, contexts, and interpretations, it is obvious that these must be considered rebuttable, that they can at best provide frameworks for analysis, and that decisions have to be made as the stream of particularities unwinds itself.

Political Leaders, State and World

Political leaders, as well as ordinary citizens, have responsibilities that go beyond the nation-state. They are citizens of the world as well as of the nation and, although they have particular responsibilities to the nation of an order not voluntarily accepted by the ordinary citizen, they ought not to ignore the impact of their actions on life styles and prospects in other nations and on hopes for a better and more viable world order. On the other hand, much of the propaganda that has been directed to young people by at least some to the effect that they should act as citizens of the world rather than as citizens of a particular nation badly misleads young people. Until such time as the nation is superseded by more enlightened and more effective forms of political organization, national values as well as world values must be pursued to a significant extent through national organizations. In this pursuit, some nations are obviously more essential than others. The extinction of Denmark, for instance, would be a cultural tragedy but the impact on humane values elsewhere might well be minimal. A serious decline in the military power and political and economic influence of the United States, however, might well have disastrous implications for many of those more enlightened values that are posited in contradistinction to nationalism. There can be occasions on which it is important for good nations to win bad wars, that is, wars entered into for particular reasons that cannot be justified according to the values of the nation or by prudential considerations. It is possible that the loss even of a bad war might threaten very important human values.

If, on the other hand, the policy of a nation threatens desirable national and international values, not merely in particular actions but in general, there is a general obligation to act against the nation. Many German citizens recognized this obligation during World War II and daringly engaged in sabotage of the activities of the Nazi regime. Precisely because the nation-state is the most effective, although not the exclusive, instrument for implementing policy in the world arena, when the national regime genuinely is a force for bad values, it is extremely important to oppose it in general even in some cases in which its policies might accomplish on balance some good.

Sometimes one hears the argument that if the government can employ force abroad without the sanction of law, it is equally valid for citizens to use force at home against injustices. Many people do believe this argument and act upon it either consciously or implicitly. There may be a relationship between the use of force abroad, at least in support of causes not fully understood by the public at large, and the breakdown of order in the domestic forum. If this is so, wise governments will endure some external risks to avoid domestic consequences injurious to the framework of values that characterizes the American polity. Yet, the argument has no validity from the moral point of view.

Although all governments attempt to suppress domestic violence, this suppression in democracies rests upon the supposition that the opportunity exists for a current minority to transform itself into a majority through persuasion. Unlike the Japanese, Americans have never accepted the notion, as given intellectual stature by John Calhoun, that particularly intense minorities have a right to block what a majority desires unless this entails a destruction of the system of majority rule itself. Although the American system of representative democracy is based upon the notion that majorities should not work their will immediately but only after delay, the underlying consensus is that majorities, if they can sustain themselves, ultimately should have their way, provided they do not attack fundamental constitutional constraints.

The international system has no such underlying consensus. It has no constitutional provisions for change. Moreover, accretions of strength for one of the actors in the system may fundamentally destabilize the system at the expense of other actors. The Baltic states found their existence destroyed by the pact between the Soviet Union and Nazi Germany. There have been significant changes in the domestic Czechoslovak system since the Soviet invasion of 1968. American intervention in Guatemala and the Dominican Republic have had major impacts upon the domestic institutions of those nations. If the United States had not intervened with great effect in World War II, albeit as the consequence of Japanese attack, we might very well be living in a world in which fascist and racist doctrines governed most of humanity. The American domestic value system is hardly immune from large-scale transformations in world politics. Whatever the wisdom or justice of American involvement in Viet Nam, the generalization that the employment of force abroad legitimatizes it at home is based upon a jejune error in analysis: the application of a generalization that applies to one kind of social system to another of a fundamentally different nature.

It would be wrong to draw the contrary inference: that force is always to be employed in the international arena and never in the domestic. The differences between the two systems, although very great in degree, do not justify such extreme inferences. There are many processes of peaceful change in the international system, including norms of internal law that are much better followed than many laymen understand, and there are sometimes circumstances even in democratic political systems in which the processes of peaceful change break down or in which the opportunity to persuade is largely formal. Yet the latter are extremely unlikely to produce a fundamental transformation of the system or to prevent rather than delay persuasion and peaceful change. The repeated threat of force, and even more the conspicuous use of force, in democratic political systems is almost surely more subversive of the processes of peaceful change than the temporary maintenance of some injustice. On the other hand, it is often only the availability of the threat of force and occasionally of the conspicuous use of force that prevents the transformation of the international system in ways that are inimical to democratic and humane values. For this reason the assertion that the use of force by the government abroad legitimates the domestic employment of force against the government is intellectually mischievous.

One other point deserves mention, although it is strongly implied in what has already been stated. The international system operates on the basis of self-help. Although it is not anarchic or lawless, whatever standards are observed are maintained through the decentralized decision making of states and through international organization. The nation operates most effectively in the international system when it acts as a coordinated and coherent unit. Its capacity to do good (or harm) is decreased to the extent that individuals and groups within the nation attempt to defeat its policies or to substitute their judgments for those of the national government. Since the hobbling of government policy rarely permits the substitution of a different and better (depending on the point of view) policy, it usually works harm even with respect to the aims of those who attack the policy decisions. The legitimation of the failure to abide by the normal methods of changing policy by changing governments at elections would destroy the consensus on the basis of which effective external policy is possible. It seems difficult to justify this, except from an exceptionally arrogant point of view, unless one is willing to make the judgment either that the government in general is evil or that a particular policy is so evil that all these other risks become acceptable. Although either conclusion might be true and although there are historical examples where each has been true, it would seem that this conclusion would not lightly be arrived at by responsible people. This would seem to be particularly true in democracies where governments must periodically submit themselves to the people.

The charge has been made that the popular will is frustrated because, for instance, there was no antiwar candidate in the 1968 elections. However, the polls showed with great consistency that Nixon was the overwhelming choice of those who considered themselves Republicans and that Humphrey was the choice of those who considered themselves Democrats. Although it is far from clear that the national will was not registered by the 1968 election regardless of party politics, this is not really essential. The electoral system is a party system and those who insist on working outside of that framework have little legitimate complaint if their influence on the process is diminished by that fact.

Justification and Conscientious Decision

Decisions with respect to state and world involve conflicts of conscience over values of overriding importance. These decisions are so important that we must be concerned not merely with the answers to which we come but with the way in which the answers are arrived at, for the justification of substantive value decisions cannot properly be divorced from the justification of the procedures by means of which they are derived. We live in a world in which information is limited, in which role responsibilities and role capabilities differ from citizen to citizen and from political leader to political leader. Although recognition of the limitation of information and responsibility when conscience genuinely demands action can be used as a rationalization for inaction, the insistence upon infallibility of judgment and the right to individual decision can become an excuse for self-righteous and irresponsible self-indulgence.

The political leader arrives at his decisions under conditions of great uncertainty. The citizen sits in judgment under conditions of great uncertainty. If their conclusions differ in ways of exceptional moral importance and if the citizen desires to consider how or whether to engage in dissent, what criteria does he apply? No set of rules can be proposed that permits an unambiguous answer. Yet, for the citizen torn between the fear that he is neglecting to dissent when moral duty requires it and the fear that he might dissent in a merely self-indulgent manner, there are at least some questions that can be asked in the effort to discover whether procedural justification is present. Does the decision adequately take into account the information that is available or is an answer leaped to on the basis of stereotyped formulas? Is there recognition that decisions are made by decision makers on the basis of information not available to the rest of the citizenry? Was there an attempt fairly to assess the motivations and aims of others and the information that might be available to them? Was the complexity of the considerations that enter into the decision and of the consequences that likely will follow from it fairly taken into account? Was there an attempt fairly to assess the consequences of opposition in situations in which one cannot change the decisions of others but might only be able to interfere with their effective implementation?

There is surely a moral difference between preventing SS storm troopers from killing Jews as efficiently as possible and interfering with the daily operations of a school because one doesn't like the program of a principal. The first genuinely accomplishes a good even though it cannot change the general policy; the latter may, although not invariably, do only harm, even to those whose interests are supposedly being protected by interfering with the educative process without replacing it by a better one.

It is part of ethical responsibility to consider consequences. For instance, much of the public dissent to the Vietnamese War needs to be related to the impact that this dissent has upon continuation of the war. Although some writers, such as Arthur Schlesinger, Jr., have argued that North Vietnamese continuation of the war is entirely unrelated to dissent within the United States and have cited some statements of Hanoi to this effect, this opinion is hardly credible and reflects seriously upon those who make it. The North Vietnamese would hardly desire to argue that their victory, if they ever do obtain one, was produced more by dissent in the United States than by their own activities. Thus they would hardly go out of their way to ascribe their success to dissent in the United States. They have on occasion denigrated the value of dissent but they have also made statements indicating the value they place upon dissent in the United States.

In any event, the North Vietnamese would be stupid indeed if their conduct of the war and of their willingness to negotiate and of the conditions under which they are willing to negotiate were not influenced by their estimate of the impact of dissent upon American official behavior. Obviously dissent is an important element both for the outcome Hanoi hopes to achieve and for the price it will have to pay to achieve it. Indeed, the North Vietnamese have often been quite open about the value they place on dissent. According to the *New York Times*:

> A Communist source noted what was called 'the realities' of the world situation, and said 'After all, we are not negotiating in a vacuum.' The principal reality, this source said, is the 'irreversible tide' of public opinion against the war in the United States including popular refusal to accept further casualties. 'They are cynical about it,' an American diplomat commented. 'They are telling us in every meeting and at every news conference that bloodshed hurts you more than it does us. If they lose 4,000 men, no one on their side knows it. If we lose 200, everyone does.' The other side also appears to be encouraged by the differences between Washington and Saigon over policy.[1]

A conscientious person might nonetheless engage in major public dissent if, in his judgment, the costs of dissent—for instance, the likely prolongation of the war—were outweighed either by other consequences that might shorten the war or by compensating gains with respect to other values injured by American intervention.

The Treatment of Dissent

A number of conflicting values enter into the treatment of dissent. It is important in a society that values autonomous choice to protect dissent. Although dissent ought not to be beyond criticism, excessive criticism of dissent runs the risk that the value of autonomous choice might be injured. However, despite much criticism of the government in this respect, it is far from clear that the latter has been the greater present danger. The factor that has been most remarkable in recent years, at least prior to the intervention of Spiro Agnew, has been the extent to which the government of the United States, with some relatively minor exceptions, has maintained a climate of opinion that protected the exercise of dissent and the extent to which the dissenters engaged in a form of reverse McCarthyism by seeking to make criticism of their activities illegitimate. The President, moreover, did have a responsibility as commander in chief of the armed forces to protect the morale of the forces in the field.

Some argue as if there should be no penalties at all for dissent. Although it is true that one desires to protect the right of reasoned speech, it is entirely unreasonable to expect that individuals will not or should not be held accountable in any way for the consequences of their speech. Sometimes some kinds of speech are genuinely inconsistent with the positions that people hold and the responsibilities that go along with the positions. For instance, if a teacher in a public school announced either in class or outside of it but publicly that Negroes are inherently inferior and cannot learn, his opinion, no matter how conscientiously held, would have an impact upon the psychologies of black youngsters that would be inconsistent with his teaching responsibilities. A similar standard would not as clearly be appropriate at the university level. A professor at a college or university, however, who advises students to come to class with guns *is* behaving in a manner inconsistent with the kind of reasoned discourse that characterizes a university; in the absence of extremely extenuating circumstances, his appointment should be terminated. Sometimes the only appropriately available penalty for speech that is injurious to important values is to hold the guilty individual up to public scorn or disgrace.

There is often a failure to distinguish the right to dissent from the right to get one's way. After the occupation of a building or the shouting down of a speaker, one often hears the argument: "But no one conceded to us when we merely engaged in talk." Yet there is no right to succeed; and it is a truism where controversy exists that some people do not like the outcome. Democracy rests on the supposition that there are appropriate institutional processes for deciding controversial issues. Suppose the Ku Klux Klan started forcibly ejecting black children from integrated schools. Would the argument that they tried talk, that they tried litigation, and that even the electoral process failed them, justify their effort? Would it really be true that the government was suppressing their dissent if it arrested them for their actions? Would their sincerity or their conscience mitigate their crime? Suppose they lynched blacks as a matter of conscience? Would that be acceptable dissent?

Sometimes speech is confused with activities that are not really speech at all. It is true that the right to dissent is not worth much if one does not have reasonable opportunities to exercise that right. Yet, is the dissenter to be the sole judge of the appropriate opportunity? Does he have the right to seize a radio station? To enter my home against my will to harangue me? Do I not have the right not to listen to him?

Suppose the Ku Klux Klan rides in sheets and on horses through the black section of a city carrying signs reading: "Black monkeys are naturally inferior and should be sent back to Africa"; "Niggers who date white women should be castrated and then lynched"; "We'll be watching every nigger who votes." Suppose a Nazi group goes through a Jewish section of town with a sign reading: "All greasy kikes should be gassed."

Are such activities merely speech? Or are they designed to intimidate and provoke? Are they related in a legitimate way to attempts to convince? Don't people have a right not to be harassed and intimidated?

Surely there is a problem here. If we merely suppress what some people dislike intensely, we may destroy meaningful dissent except within a very narrow range of options. Limitations on dissent can, and in some places will, be misused to undermine it. There is a conflict of principles here for which no perfect solution is possible. Moreover, we should attempt to avoid equating planned group provocations with spontaneous individual quarrels in justifying action against one who takes a provocatory position.

Yet surely it should not be beyond the ingenuity of our legislative and judicial systems to devise rules and regulations reasonably protective of both the right to exercise dissent and the right not to be provocatively harassed. Such extreme provocatory harassment is itself destructive of the civility required for constitutional order. The example it sets is destructive of the political community and poisons democratic consensus. If people have a right to prejudice and to express their prejudices— and I believe they do—they are nonetheless not merely indulging in verbal dissent when they manifest the behavior described above. Any reasonable man knows this and so do those who engage in such provocatory behavior. Such behavior is not in any major or legitimate way part of an effort to communicate a political doctrine. It is designed directly, rather than indirectly, to produce action and likely violence. Whatever the abstract and absolutist interpretation of the first amendment made by the Supreme Court, we have the right—even more, the duty—to protect the polity against this.

There are times, however, when I suspect that many so-called liberals do not really believe in dissent or the value of criticism but instead are merely advocates of particular substantive positions. Was Senator Eugene McCarthy, for instance, merely making a disinterested observation after Secretary of Agriculture Orville Freeman was hooted down at the University of Wisconsin when he said that if administration spokesmen wish to be heard, they should stay away from college campuses? Was he appealing to reason during the New Hampshire primary in 1968 when he accused administration supporters of (Joe) McCarthyism for stating that Moscow would be pleased if he won? "Joe McCarthyism," I had thought, implied a reckless profusion of false charges. Although it would be deplorable if we let Moscow's likes and dislikes determine America's actions, surely the contention was relevant and, as reports from Russia established after the primary, accurate. Who was guilty of a profusion of false charges? More recently (November 1969), a returned prisoner of war, Major James Rowe, declared that American POW's largely ignored Hanoi's propaganda until late 1967, when

Hanoi began citing U.S. Senators by name. "The peace demonstrators and the disheartening words of these Senators made our life more difficult," said Major Rowe. Although appropriate national interests may require such consequences, surely Major Rowe has a right and a direct personal interest in challenging this. Note, however, the libertarian concern of Senator Stephen Young of Ohio for Major Rowe. "Major Rowe," Young said, "should be silenced or assigned to some other post of duty outside Washington. A tour in the Aleutian Islands or some post in remote Turkey might cause his mouthings to be silenced."[2] Whether the Department of Defense assigned Major Rowe to the Washington area because of his views—an improper action— or whether his assignment was independent of his views, the motives of Senator Young and of his "liberal" cohorts were transparent. They were making a brutal use of the powers of the Senate in an effort to stifle criticism.

Notes

1. *New York Times* (June 25, 1969).
2. *Chicago Daily News* (November 29-30, 1969).

5   Perspectives on Self-Determination, Intervention, and Force

The basic principles of political obligation have received more attention in the three preceding chapters than they will receive in the three that follow. Although both sets of chapters deal with specific issues in the polity in the context of principle, the subject matter of the next three chapters will touch directly on matters of principle much less often. For the most part the principles that govern obligation have already been stated and the greater need is to consider the questions of foreign and military policy to which principled objections, amounting to a claim of illegitimacy, have been raised.

The purpose of this chapter is to raise serious questions concerning self-determination, intervention, and force. The failure to ask good questions or to make good analytical distinctions often leads to an apparent contest over values and principles where much of the real dispute may be over the character of the world, the availability of choices, or the consequences of making them. Although Talleyrand was said to view a mistake as worse than a crime, it may still be worthwhile to distinguish between the two. Perhaps a sufficiently mistaken government may be responsible for worse atrocities than an immoral one and thus may require even more determined opposition. Yet, at least this distinction does permit us to examine the nature of the world, whereas if irreconcilable principles are believed to be involved, it may be difficult even to gain attention for a factual inquiry. I propose to examine problems of intervention, of bargaining with Communists, of ballistic missile defense, and of foreign policy alternatives, to at least indicate the possibility that questions of fact and of interpretation, and not only of principle, may be involved. These, then, constitute the subject matters of this and the two following chapters.

This chapter primarily raises questions, and it does this to establish that much of the rhetoric over intervention is demagogic at worst or fails to consider the subject analytically at best. The chapter on dealing with Communists is designed to remove that subject from the Alice-in-Wonderland aspects that usually govern it to one of difficult choices in a competitive world. The discussion of ballistic missile defense is designed to show that the subject of the arms race cannot be dismissed with the usual clichés concerning an industrial-military complex. Defense questions do constitute an intrinsic problem in the contemporary world and, although people may differ legitimately about their resolution, it does not follow that the advocates of new military systems are necessarily wrong, inherently immoral, desirous of conflict, opposed to reasonable arms control measures, or in favor of "overkill," a much abused term.

Much of the opposition to American policy is based on the view that the government is not trying to build a better world. I do not care to be put into the position of defending specific governmental policies, when I disapprove of many. But it is useful to sketch some of the larger contours of world politics and some of the alternatives in world futures and in national policies that may present themselves, as well as one possible macrodesign for American policy as is done in Chapter 7.

National Self-Determination

If autonomy is a desirable value for the individual, is self-determination an equally desirable value for the political unit? Even if we leave out of account units that are obviously too small, too poor, or too weak to be genuinely self-governing in the present world system, and if we recognize that political organizations, as is true of individuals, are subject to external influences, there are still serious questions as to what is meant by self-determination. Does a successful revolution by a small group of determined revolutionaries in a colonial area constitute self-determination? What of the great mass of individuals who have been passive in the process and who were not consulted during it? Is there less self-determination under a colonial regime that permits some democratic parliamentary procedures or under a totalitarian domestic dictatorship? Does majority voting on Cyprus constitute self-determination when a substantial minority, the Turks, consider themselves with some justice to be oppressed by a cohesive majority? Is self-determination denied when Mozambique is made part of metropolitan Portugal? Would the fact that only a few blacks are franchised in Mozambique matter if the franchise were genuinely open to all who qualified and if qualification were reasonably open to all who aspired thereto? Does rule by one group over another become imperialistic when both groups, or only one, or either, regard the groups as fundamentally distinguished according to some important characteristic? Could a situation become imperialistic that was not previously so? Could the racial issue in the United States partake of this characteristic in time? Obviously the use of such terms over time can change as certain situations in particular contexts appear either more or less similar.

Some of the situations alluded to involve elements of tragedy that are hidden by the rhetoric of our age. The South Africans, for instance, are in a dilemma. The whites of that unhappy nation have no place, even if they desired one, to emigrate to and face a bleak future if they accede to a one-man, one-vote common franchise. The advice being offered them so cavalierly is unrealistic and even unjust. They are not admirable people but their managerial skills did build the nation and it will be taken from them under majority rule. On the other hand, their efforts to maintain control have forced them increasingly, and not clearly unwillingly, to repressive and fascistic actions that denigrate the dignity both of blacks and of whites in South Africa. The situation would not be tragic if there were a reasonable solution; it is the fact that almost any alternative involves massive costs for one group or the other that makes the situation tragic.

The Rhodesian situation might have been more manageable, but efforts to cast the problem in terms of democratic rule have been less than enlightening. Democracy and majority rule rest upon the concept of consensus—consensus on values and on procedures—and upon the minimal substratum of experience and socialization necessary for democratic values to become firmly established. A rapid movement toward majority rule in Rhodesia almost surely would produce the same authoritarianism it has produced in most of the rest of Africa. The white Rhodesians are well aware of this. It is absurd to ask that they do in the name of democracy what would prove destructive of the limited democracy that now exists in Rhodesia. Unfortunately, whatever possibility might have existed for a gradual transfer of authority as blacks were acculturated to the modern economy and society was gravely damaged by Harold Wilson's flamboyant domestic political use of the issue. The original proposal for a commission, with the Chief Justice of Rhodesia sitting as chairman, might have produced a sensible gradualist document that might possibly have been accepted in Rhodesia. That opportunity was bypassed because of Wilson's politicking and the extremely ideological approach within the United Nations. Since then there has been a radicalization of the situation in Rhodesia that will likely lead to many, if not to all, of the repressive and racist types of legislation found in South Africa.

What is so dreadfully depressing about the Rhodesian problem is not that it could have been solved, for one cannot know that, but that the agencies that might have played a constructive role in the situation instead helped exacerbate it. In both South Africa and Rhodesia, it now appears that whatever occurs will involve major damage for at least one and possibly both of the groups involved in conflict. Nonetheless, it is essential that American distaste for the unjust situations in South Africa and Rhodesia be kept clear. If cavalier, hypocritical advice ought to be avoided, it is even more important to avoid condoning the evils of racism.

The rhetoric of our time is depressing. Premier Olaf Palme of Sweden has stated that he has "absolutely more sympathy" for the North Vietnamese government than for the government in Saigon. "North Vietnam," he said, "is a dictatorship. . . but is representative of the people." The Saigon regime is "not representative but speaks for a relatively small clique."[1] Apart from his dubious "facts," would Premier Palme have had "absolute sympathy" for the Nazi regime because it was representative? Is it the degree of support or the values represented by a regime or the consequences of its existence, as contrasted with alternatives that should be considered more important? Premier Palme represents a demagogic corruption of democratic beliefs that heralds ill for the age in which we live.

The Right of Intervention

How far does the right of international intervention or of influence by external forces go? The "balance of power" system put strong limitations on the right of intervention; the loose bipolar system and the system or systems evolving from it put fewer restrictions on this right. Even so, it is obvious that unlimited intervention would be inconsistent with maintaining at least a minimum of international order.

Is intervention permissible where the request is made by a formally installed and recognized government? Such intervention would cover the cases of Viet Nam and the Dominican Republic. In the Dominican Republic, the intervention quickly stabilized the situation and permitted withdrawal. In Viet Nam, the United States has not yet been able to withdraw and, until recently, was taking over an increasing share of the burden of defending the government against the revolutionaries. Is there some upper limit beyond which intervention becomes external rule and not merely a matter of helping an indigenous government stabilize itself against internal foes aided by external enemies?

If we adopt a criterion for the right of intervention that would depend upon a formal request by a legitimately recognized government and that would be related to the ability of that government to extend and then to maintain its control in the area, would we then have argued against intervention in Nazi Germany after Hitler's accession to power in 1933 or the Rhineland reoccupation of 1936? Yet, had intervention occurred then, most authorities believe that World War II almost surely would have been avoided.

Suppose a regime engages in genocide or in other brutal activities. Are there then any conditions under which intervention can be justified? Obviously, we are again confronted with a situation in which particular principles can carry us only so far and in which they have to be balanced against other values and principles.

Has the situation gone so far in the case of Haiti that we would be willing to pay a price in terms of international order and the norms governing it to remove Duvalier? The situation is not as bad as genocide, and Haiti is not a major threat to international order. Perhaps, in such cases, one ought to wait until it is possible to use the technique employed in the Dominican Republic after the assassination of Trujillo, when the American fleet stood offshore as a symbol to internal political forces that the United States wanted major democratic changes. Perhaps the United States can intervene successfully without an invitation if conditions permit it to use fictions as in Guatemala in 1954 or Iran in 1953.

Such fictions maintain a façade that is less destructive to international values than open military intervention, as the Red Chinese fiction of volunteers made clear in Korea in 1950. The example of the Bay of Pigs in Cuba also illustrates that one cannot wait too long in using these fictions. What might have been acceptable within the framework of international order had it worked in 1961 would by 1963 have become an anachronism, an onslaught against an established government that would have been deeply shocking to international values. Perhaps the Israelis would have fared better in world opinion in January, 1969, if they had employed a fiction, albeit a transparent one, in the attack on the Beirut Airport.

What of the direct use of military force when not invited by the local government? Such interventions obviously shock international expectations and values in a major way. Perhaps, however, they can be successfully employed as in Hungary in 1956, when an alternative government was available, or Czechoslovakia in 1968, when the Czechoslovak Communist Party could be manipulated to legitimate retroactively certain aspects of the invasion. In these cases, even if international norms are somewhat damaged, the damage remains limited.

The combination of norms, values, means of influence, instruments of control, international context, and so forth, that is relevant to decisions will change from circumstance to circumstance and from case to case, although the precedential value of decisions has also to be taken into account. Perhaps the most that one can say is that the presumption should be against direct military intervention, except where a request is made by a legitimate and recognized government. This presumption, however, is rebuttable, depending upon circumstances.

The Use of Force

The United Nations Charter contains provisions against the use of force except in self-defense. It has been maintained by this writer repeatedly that this provision misjudges the nature of the international system in which the norm is to be applied and runs the risk, if taken seriously, of undermining those controls that can be placed upon the use of force in favor of an outright prohibition that is unenforceable.

When Russia attacked Finland in 1940, the natural sympathies of the world went to brave little Finland. But it was obvious from a Russian perspective that Leningrad required greater defense in depth than it had, and that the security of the Soviet Union might depend upon a more defensible border. Although perhaps the Russians made a strategic mistake in attacking Finland, it is naive to believe that a responsible Russian leadership would have failed, on grounds of principle, to use the means available to it, and usable by it given the authoritarian nature of the regime, to protect Russian security.

Until 1954, Israel had a strategy of absorbing an Arab attack and then striking back. With the acquisition of fast jet aircraft and modern tanks by Arab armies, the Israelis were required by elementary prudence to shift their strategy. If the Arabs massed, for instance, in the Gaza strip, a maneuver that is useful only for attack and not for defense, it was urgent for the Israelis to strike first under the new conditions. This they did in 1956 and 1967.

It has since been argued that Israeli success on both occasions established that there was no need for the attacks. This assertion is nonsense. The Israelis suffered proportionately more casualties in the five-day 1967 war than the United States has suffered in Viet Nam; yet these costs of the war weigh heavily on the American mentality. Moreover, the Israeli success after a first strike, including the incapacitation of Egyptian planes and airfields, is no precedent for what might have happened had the Arabs struck first. An Arab first strike would surely have been more difficult to handle and much more costly in terms of human life; it is questionable that Israel would hold the favorable vantage points she now holds had the Arabs struck first. It is not inconceivable that the Arabs might have held some Israeli territory when the war terminated or that the war might have lasted longer. During a longer war extensive Russian aid might have reached the Arabs. Moreover, the Israelis are incapable of fighting a long war and maintaining their economy at the same time. These possibilities are not so small that a prudent Israeli leadership can afford to leave them out of account. Joint American and Soviet pressures might have forced the Israelis not to strike or to retreat or even to accept a minor defeat that might have led to a pessimistic prognosis for Israel's future. However, the present international system does not provide striking incentives for observance of Charter norms on the use of force. The failure of the United Nations to denounce Israel as an aggressor constitutes a partial implicit recognition of the inadequacy of the norms of the Charter.

Notes
1. *New York Times* (October 15, 1969).

6   Perspectives on Bargaining with Communists and Arms Races

Bargaining with Communists

Even though only rebuttable perspectives can be offered concerning bargaining with Communists, some perspectives are better than others in terms of accounting for the events of the past. The *New York Times,* which is hardly noted for the acuity of its editorial perspectives, gave Arthur Schlesinger, Jr. editorial space to develop the theme that Ho Chi Minh was irrational and therefore so inflexibly wedded to certain objectives that he would pursue them regardless of the costs that the United States imposed upon him. James Reston, also utilizing the editorial page of the *New York Times,* pointed out that one important reason for voting against Nixon was that the Russians were so suspicious of him that they would be unwilling to negotiate with him. Many speak of the irrationality of Mao Tse-tung. Others have since written learned themes on the paranoiac tendencies of Josef Stalin.

One wonders whether actual psychotics are as inflexible or as insensitive to cost considerations as are Communist leaders according to some of our learned pundits. One wonders how one can live in a world with such leaders except by conceding to them whatever their contemporary demands happen to be. Even genuine paranoids, however, do have their cost calculi, although it is sometimes difficult to fathom just what they happen to be. And there is much in the history of diplomatic bargaining procedures, as they have manifested themselves over time, to indicate that Communist leaders, who might just happen not to be paranoid or totally irrational, do tend to be more calculating and less sentimental bargainers than Western statesmen.

Much of what appears to some as examples of irrationality in Communist systems, and which perhaps in part may be related to some personality aberrations, lies in a purge cycle that may result more from certain system constraints than from personality inputs. In Russia, in China, and in Burma, we find that Communist purges begin, they intensify, they turn on those who initially carried them out, and then they moderate. Without examining this process in any detail, it appears quite plausible that a combination of revolutionary goals and requirements of regime control lead to the initiation of purges and then that a cycle of consequences is set in motion that may differ in its severity from place to place and from condition to condition. Part of this purge process may depend upon personality inputs, but the general character of the process remains relatively constant, leading to the inference that more general system factors are responsible.

Communist bargaining tactics in the Vietnamese case are consistent with those the Russians have engaged in, those the Chinese have engaged in, and with negotiations during the final stages of the Korean War. There is apparently a general style of Communist bargaining that is related to their concept of conflict, to their view of history, to their estimates concerning the weaknesses of the Western world, and to at least an implicit theory of the bargaining process. No doubt there are also variations produced by national culture, individual temperament, and circumstance; but little has systematically been explicated about these.

In general, Communist bargainers are extremely tough, obdurate, reluctant to make concessions from weakness except when forced, adaptive to changed circumstances, skillful in the psychological manipulation of adversaries and in exhausting them in protracted negotiations. Although apparently capable of responding to individual differences among Western negotiators, Communist negotiators apparently see themselves as the representatives of an impersonal process that sustains and gives direction to their efforts. Although ready to use the good will of adversaries, they place no reliance upon the consistency of such good will and inherently suspect it. They apparently feel safer when the points of conflict are obvious than when the other side proclaims a harmony of interest that is inconsistent with the dialectic in which they ultimately believe. Nonetheless they are usually supremely pragmatic. They understand that there are temporary coincidences of interest superimposed upon more deep-seated and longer-lasting conflicts and that these temporary coincidences of interest permit temporary agreements and adjustments. They also understand that, under pressure, concessions are necessary that are consistent with the temporary balancing forces and smaller than the costs of alternative policies.

They will seize upon every ambiguity or loophole in temporary agreements to evade them. They will also attempt to make these violations of either the spirit or the letter of the agreements sufficiently ambiguous to deter the other side from rupturing the agreement completely as long as this is advantageous to them. They will attempt to reach agreements that maximize their opportunities either to evade agreements or to use them for ulterior purposes.

All things change and perhaps some day Communist bargaining styles will change or a Communist leader will arise who fails to follow the style. Nonetheless, until considerable evidence arises that such is the case, the presumption continues to favor the orientation that has just been offered.

A contrasting opinion is offered by Senator Fulbright. Although Senator Fulbright and his consulting psychiatrist, Dr. Jerome Frank, believe that the way to reach agreement with the Russians is to behave toward them in a friendly fashion, to the extent that Russian bargaining behavior is complicated by their indigenous suspiciousness, Russian leaders apparently tend to be more suspicious of the gifts offered by liberals than of the deals offered by conservatives. This was strikingly illustrated by the remark of the Underkommissar of the Narkomindel, Potemkin, to the French Ambassador, Coulandre, the day after the Munich pact was signed: "Ah, my poor friend, this means the fourth partition of Poland." The vituperation of the Berlin radio and the existence of the anti-Comintern pact among the Axis powers did not convince the Russians that a deal with Germany was impossible. On the contrary, they anticipated that they could strike a bargain, and they were right.

It was the Western leadership that was credulous, that was unable to believe that the Soviet Union either would desire to or would be able to strike a bargain with the Axis powers. Then, when the bargain was struck, we developed the theory that both totalitarianisms were similar and therefore that the countries were natural partners. Thus, England made an effort to come to the aid of Finland during the winter war of 1940, an effort that if successful would have forced Russia into the war on the German side. Most Western observers failed to note that the Soviet work week was increased immediately after Paris fell to the Germans. Very few Western observers understood that Soviet moves in the Baltic and in Eastern Europe were designed to secure space against a German attack. And to this day many Western observers tend to misinterpret the measures Stalin took in a desperate effort to delay the German attack as evidence that Stalin did not believe in the possibility of an attack. He did, apparently, reject the claim that the attack would occur approximately when it did.

The inability of the critics of the Johnson administration to understand Communist bargaining practices is apparently an indication of a much deeper failure to understand the nature of international politics and of international bargaining. Many of the same people who denounce the Johnson administration denounced the South Vietnamese government when it apparently rejected the American-North Vietnamese agreement for substantive negotiations in Paris. Apart from displaying the arrogance that they usually accuse others of, these people also overlooked the fact that the apparent rejection by the South Vietnamese government served a number of important political functions: it met the fears of many in South Viet Nam that the government might cooperate in an American sellout; it served to reinforce the impression that the South Vietnamese government was not an American puppet but was instead an independent decision-making body; it served notice on the United States that it could not negotiate substantively without taking into account the political goals of the South Vietnamese government. Much of the irritation with the slowness of the bargaining in Paris fails to take into account that this slowness is not merely a matter of face but has deep political implications. It permits testing the will and straining the patience of the other side; it permits, for example, consolidation of one's own position or re-enforcing the morale of the troops in the field.

Of course, not all apparently naive attacks upon this process are genuinely naive; they can also have the political function of affecting the negotiations. Nonetheless, one gets the impression that most of the critics do not use their remarks functionally but that instead their remarks manifest ignorance of the bargaining process. Many of their activities are quite counterproductive, as would have been the case had the so-called doves succeeded in affecting in a major way the Democratic party platform on the subject of Viet Nam in Chicago in 1968. The dove plank might have delayed negotiations, by raising the prospect of greater future concessions. Victory for the Democratic nominee after the adoption of such a platform might have turned into a bargaining disaster for him as a consequence of North Vietnamese expectations based on a plank that an incumbent president could have accommodated only at the cost of major foreign policy objectives.

During the Viet Nam negotiations, there have been many demands that the United States make certain concessions; for instance, Senator McCarthy's demand that the United States concede a coalition government before entering the negotiations or that the bombing be halted unconditionally. Without discussing the substantive defects of the proposition that a coalition government be conceded unilaterally, it is nonetheless appropriate to analyze the inadequacies of the underlying conception of the negotiation process that is apparently revealed by such a demand. Concessions must not be offered too soon, for this leaves one without anything to bargain with when seeking concessions from the other side. There have even been occasions when American newspapers have announced that such and such is the public American position in a negotiation but that something else is the fallback position. Such a revelation immediately establishes the fallback position as the initial negotiating position. Little could be worse for securing successful negotiations. Although there are occasions on which an initial unilateral concession might prove useful, this is an extremely delicate business and one that many Americans seem to lack comprehension of.

Similar misconceptions governed dove statements on the issue of a bombing halt. Although the attitude of the North Vietnamese toward winning the insurrection in the south is obviously based on values and objectives more central to them than are our corresponding American attitudes to us, and although the North Vietnamese are probably much more willing to accept higher human costs than are Americans, it is a pathetic fallacy to believe that the demands they were making with respect to the halting of the bombing were irrational and thus unresponsive to American policy and public postures. If many of the American measures designed to bring pressure upon the North Vietnamese were based on mistaken estimates, the conclusion on the part of some commentators, including Senator Eugene McCarthy, that the North Vietnamese had therefore demonstrated their refusal to negotiate except on their terms is now revealed, although there should never have been any question about it, as a misperception of what was a bargaining strategy.

The terms under which parties to negotiations enter into negotiations have an effect on the course of negotiations. To have accepted the North Vietnamese terms would have been a sign to the South Vietnamese that the Americans were prepared to make major concessions threatening to the futures of non-Communist South Vietnamese. This would have set in chain a number of circumstances in South Viet Nam that would further have re-enforced North Viet Nam's bargaining power. Such concessions would have been a sign to America's allies that America was responsive to pressures for concessions and such pressures would have been multiplied by them as the negotiations continued. Acceptance of North Vietnamese demands in the form in which they were offered would have constituted an internal sign to the American delegation that likely would have produced an erosion of its will. It is unlikely that the North Vietnamese were not fully aware of these factors and it is likely that their stance was adopted in part at least to exploit them. On the other hand, after having stated their demands so explicitly and continuously for so long a period, explicit retreat from them by the North Vietnamese would have been a sign to their own cadres in the south that would have lowered their morale.

Acceptance of the compromise that was reached at Paris probably reflected certain weaknesses in the northern military position after the failure of the Tet offensive and perhaps also an attempt to influence the American elections by bringing in a presidential candidate who would be more responsive to concessions, or a recognition that neither candidate would make the concessions that they had once hoped for, or a desire to begin serious negotiations before the Johnson regime went out of office. These alternative inferences are quite speculative and one would do well not to place too much weight on them. Moreover, the Communists did seize upon the American need for an agreement to achieve one that was a masterpiece of ambiguity.

It is not entirely clear that the interests of the negotiating parties at Paris can be compromised sufficiently to produce a negotiated solution—as opposed to tacitly reduced commitments by both Hanoi and Washington—to the war in South Viet Nam. What the episode conclusively demonstrates is not that the Johnson administration had the correct foreign policy objectives but that it had a far better understanding of the process of negotiating with Communists than most of its opponents.

The Johnson administration was dealing with people from a vastly different culture that was imbedded in a political, military, and economic context of which it had only a poor understanding. The Johnson administration therefore might have misjudged numerous details any one of which could have been crucial to the process of negotiation. Nonetheless it understood much better than did its opponents the general character of the bargaining process in which it was engaged.

The moratorium and its consequences might have forced the Nixon administration into an untenable bargaining position, much as Johnson was undercut. It is unfortunate that so much pressure was being placed upon the American government for precipitate withdrawal at a time when the war was in the process of being won and when the Nixon administration was committed to a timely withdrawal. According to the *New York Times* of November 3, 1969—a newspaper thoroughly sceptical concerning the war—"the belief that things are going well is shared, moreover, by the most experienced officers in Vietnam, many of whom built their reputations here as iconoclasts and pessimists." Although the administration must share the blame, for reason of its credibility gap, only the gods could take pleasure in the irony that the critics disbelieve their political victory so thoroughly that many of them are willing to sacrifice all the blood and suffering of the war to cast a fetter on their own government.

Arms Race Perspectives and Military Bargaining

Is military superiority meaningless in a world in which both nuclear superpowers can inflict immense damage upon the other in a second strike? What are the uncertainties? How good is our intelligence? Soviet missiles in Cuba were emplaced very rapidly. Our discovery of this build-up would not have been likely in the absence of almost continuous surveillance techniques, and these were then possible only because Cuba was a mere ninety miles from our shores. Although SAMOS is excellent, it is likely not as good a surveillance means. Could the Soviet Union stockpile large numbers of nuclear weapons and then emplace them so rapidly that we could not overcome their lead time?

Mr. McNamara has stated his confidence that American intelligence can protect against the danger that the Soviet Union can obtain secretly a significant strategic edge. Such intelligence would consist of evidence from SAMOS, clandestine intelligence, and budgetary intelligence. Is not the Cuban case a counter-example for this claim? Have not advances in the miniaturization of warheads diminished the value of the first two kinds of intelligence? Have not Soviet camouflage advances reinforced this conclusion? Does not the introduction of MIRV and other qualitative advances increase these uncertainties enormously? Given the numerous ways of disguising expenditures in the Soviet budget, how much confidence can be placed in budgetary intelligence? Did not the firm estimates of Soviet missile strength issued by the Department of Defense under McNamara hide major uncertainties?

Consider the mistakes at the time of Pearl Harbor. Torpedoes were not supposed to explode in shallow water and the Japanese Zeroes were not supposed to have as much range as they had for the attack. The Navy concluded in late 1968 that the Scorpion was not sunk by enemy attack because there was no external explosion. Although I do not want to argue that its conclusion concerning a possible enemy attack was wrong or that the two French and the Israeli vessels or some unreported others were sunk by enemy attack, for this hardly seems the most likely alternative, I know of at least one plausible method by means of which such vessels can be sunk without external explosion or warning. Perhaps the Department of Defense suffers from excessive self-confidence, a self-confidence that hardly seems warranted given the number of major blunders that it has made.

Could qualitative changes in the arms race, FOBS (Fractional Orbital Ballistic Satellites), orbital weapons, MIRV (Multiple Independent Reentry Vehicles), ballistic missile defenses, and ASW (Anti-Submarine Warfare) breakthroughs change the strategic balance in a significant way? Could this be done before adequate intelligence permits countermeasures? Are such strategic changes of significance even if the United States would not be deprived of the capability of doing considerable damage to the Soviet Union in a second strike?

The CIA has hardly distinguished itself by its role in helping to cast the National Intelligence Estimates. Before 1961, it consistently overestimated Soviet strategic strength. Since 1961, it has consistently underestimated Soviet strategic strength, although most of its blunders have been obscured by self-serving secrecy classifications. It is now well known that contrary to firm CIA estimates the Soviets have been developing a new strategic bomber. It is not public knowledge that since 1961 the CIA has consistently and radically failed in its strength projections for one Soviet strategic system; yet it has never seen fit to question its methods. There have been no atmospheric tests since 1963 and therefore we have no observational intelligence on Soviet warhead megatonnage. According to known technologies, one particular class of Soviet strategic missiles could carry from x to 4x megatons. Yet the CIA presents its estimate of x megatons as if it were based on hard intelligence. The estimates on Soviet missile accuracy are subject to Soviet attempts at deception. Although there are several methods for estimating accuracy and although deception would be difficult with respect to some, this is possible and the Soviets are known to be highly secretive. Yet the CIA presents its figures as if they were trustworthy. More recently the Soviet Union has attempted to disguise even the fact that it was testing strategic weapons.

The problem of intelligence concerning Soviet MIRV is particularly serious. For a long period of time, it was believed that the Soviet Union had tested only a MRV, that is, a missile the warheads of which were not independently maneuverable. Then it was noticed that the pattern of attack was similar to that of Minutemen placement and that the Soviet bus was large enough so that, unlike the case of American MIRV weapons, the guidance systems of the Soviet warheads could be self-contained. Moreover, the Soviet weapons are powerful enough to be useful against hardened sites, whereas the smaller American warheads are not useful except against cities, at least until much more precise accuracies are achieved—perhaps in the late 1970's or the 1980's. Unfortunately for arms control purposes, it does not seem possible to know which of the competing hypotheses concerning Soviet MIRV is correct.

The Soviet Union has a much greater variety of strategic

weapons than has the United States and we have not yet de-
ciphered their purpose. They have continued to expand their
ICBM installations beyond parity and CIA estimates. Yet
their capacity for a first strike against the United States—we will
barely advert to this later—is greater than that projected by
Secretary Laird even if one accepts the unreliable CIA estimates.
The leading Soviet military journal, *Red Star,* carries articles
which advocate a pre-emptive nuclear first strike in anticipation
of attack and declare that nuclear wars can be won. The CIA
does not consider the possibility that its intelligence estimates,
which are really based on political and strategic assumptions
concerning Soviet motivations, might be mistaken on both
grounds. Yet, as will be argued, the strategic considerations
behind apparent Soviet planning might be well conceived—particularly their counterforce targeting, as contrasted with Mc-
Namara's population targeting.

Suppose—although I hardly consider this a likely contin-
gency—the Soviet Union did make a disarming strike against
the United States that was reasonably successful in damaging
American counterforce capabilities but quite limited in terms
of civilian damage. Would the United States then strike at
major Soviet cities with its remaining limited strategic forces
even though the Soviet Union would have enough strategic force
in reserve to obliterate the United States? Or would the United
States accept a limited defeat?

It is a mistake to believe that strategic forces are useful
only in massive military strikes or that they play no role in political bargaining in crisis. Would it make no difference, for instance, if the Soviet Union invaded Yugoslavia with superior
conventional forces, whether the United States or the Soviet
Union had strategic superiority in nuclear weapons? If, for
instance, there were a strategic nuclear exchange at a low level—
a demonstration strike, a limited retaliatory strike, or a limited
counterforce strike—and if neither side were willing to risk
higher levels of exchange, might not the side that won at the
low level of exchange be deemed to have "won" in some sense
that would affect the political bargaining that followed?

It is, however, not necessary that a strategic superiority be used for it to make a difference. It is difficult to believe that differences in strategic strength will not affect the bargaining power of states in a crisis by influencing their expectations. The militarily stronger side need not win. Situational advantages, political and economic factors, skill in bargaining, political will, and reputation will also influence the result. Everything else being equal, however, it likely would be a mistake to deny the importance of at least some kinds and degrees of strategic superiority.

It is difficult to believe that American resolution at the time of the Cuban missile crisis was not improved as a consequence of American nuclear strategic superiority (in addition to local conventional dominance). The prospect that the Soviet Union might have taken provocative counteractions elsewhere in the world had they possessed strategic superiority or parity cannot be prudently discounted by a responsible decision maker.

This is not an assertion of a fact—namely, that the Soviet Union would have moved against Berlin, for instance, if the Soviet Union had had the strategic advantage at the time of the Cuban missile crisis that Secretary of Defense Laird projects for 1974. The argument does imply, however, that such differences in strategic posture will be among the important considerations taken into account by Soviet decision makers in determining policy and that therefore they must be among the important considerations taken into account by American decision makers in providing a force structure that damps the likelihood that a crisis will be either deliberately created or deliberately escalated by Russia. It is also interesting that the big Soviet missile build-up was apparently planned just after the Cuban missile crisis, perhaps suggesting that the American strategic nuclear advantage did play a significant role in the outcome.

Nuclear systems are notoriously complex and are untested in part, except in computer simulations. Although very complex systems, partly tested by computer simulation, such as Apollo, have worked, it is extremely unlikely that the Soviet Union would employ such a high-risk strategy as a first strike. Yet can this possibility safely be entirely discounted? Any nuclear war—and especially a losing one—would do awesome damage to the United States. We cannot neglect the possibility that an intense international crisis—perhaps a conventional war in Europe—combined with a regime crisis in the Soviet Union might make even the risks of a first strike seem less to the Soviet leadership than those of a failure to employ it if the United States strategic system were vulnerable. Moreover, in such a crisis a Soviet attack might be viewed as pre-emptive and thus as consistent with Soviet declaratory policy. Therefore one might prefer the costs of an arms posture that would so increase the risks that it would almost surely rule out a Soviet first strike, short of an insane leadership in Russia. Moreover, if one considers the concessions that the United States might be forced into in circumstances in which the Russian incentives were so high and the American vulnerabilities so great, these also might justify the costs of a less vulnerable arms posture.

A thin ballistic missile defense system (BMD) represents an effort to avoid the vulnerabilities inherent in Minuteman. Although some aspects of this problem can be discussed in general without detailed knowledge of the specific characteristics of the weapons system and of interchange characteristics, these do not permit any kind of firm conclusion with respect to the installation of a particular system. Policy in this case can only be based on detailed weapons information that is classified. Much of this classification is, in the author's opinion, unjustified on grounds of military security. Moreover, the data presented in McNamara's posture statements are somewhat misleading. As a consequence it is possible to make only sparing *ex cathedra* statements.

Ballistic missile defense is one of the best researched weapons systems the United States has ever developed. Significant aspects of BMD have been tested, although obviously no BMD system has been tested as a whole. The remarks I make about BMD must be qualified by the recognition that I have not checked independently the BMD system parameters on which my conclusions are based or the sensitivity of the system design to changes in these parameters. Moreover, my remarks are not intended as a comment upon the specific features proposed for Safeguard. Nonetheless, it appears extremely likely that a ballistic missile defense system of a size up to some upper limit is dollar-for-dollar a more efficient expenditure than the same sum put into offensive missiles, and more efficient at the margin in an offense-defense race, unless the United States intends to strike first in a full-scale nuclear exchange; there are some compensating advantages for the expenditure even in the case in which the United States strikes first.

A thin BMD system is believed to be capable of preventing penetration in the case in which a small nuclear power attacks with as many as several hundred ICBM's. Even if it turns out to be not that good, it would still establish an extremely effective deterrent posture. Despite the state of research in the nuclear weapons area, we do not know whether either offensive or defensive systems will work in large interchanges under combat conditions. Yet there have been a number of occasions in the past when BMD systems might have worked much better than anyone claimed. Effects such as neutrons, hard x rays, soft x rays, and gamma rays might have incapacitated virtually all incoming missiles. When such effects are known, they can usually be designed against (although at a cost). One cannot assume that there is not a yet undiscovered effect. A nation that did not have BMD would have to assume that one possessing such a system might be able to achieve nearly perfect defensive results; this would likely play a major role in crisis negotiations or war. Moreover, it is wrong to assume that even known effects are designed against. This is not always done and, even when it is done, quite often there is a significant time gap. Much money and effort are required. Even the simplest penetration aids, such as chaff, are enormously difficult—and enormously expensive—to develop usefully. Such design adaptation is a major problem for the United States, let alone for the Soviet Union or especially for China. Moreover, if we do not remain in the BMD business, we will not acquire the necessary knowledge.

It is questionable, if BMD installation were to be halted, whether needed scientific personnel can be retained in research.

The advantages of BMD, however, are not restricted to large interchanges. BMD protects against small counterforce strikes by a major power that might be afraid to make a larger strike that would do so much civilian damage that a retaliatory strike could not be avoided. It guards against some dangers arising from the cases of accidental, unauthorized, and inadvertent small attacks. It provides against dangerous asymmetries in the area of demonstration or limited retaliatory attacks. It reduces casualties in large nuclear wars and it improves relative outcomes. It avoids the instabilities of strategic response upon possibly faulty radar indications. By permitting a defensive response only, it avoids the possible transformation of system errors or of limited attacks into a holocaust in those circumstances in which the nuclear "balance" has again become delicate—a condition we seem to be approaching with some of the qualitative offensive weapons developments.

Contrary to some claims, the system does not invite attack, except in some cases in which the attacker desires to do damage to civilians; in those cases, the fact that the BMD system invites attack reduces the potential damage that can be done in an attack of any given size. Similar reasons support the installation of short-range Sprints for the protection of the strategic forces. Some qualifications would be made if a detailed study could be presented but these would not significantly affect the major arguments. The danger of accidental explosion is insignificant. There might be an arms race. However, there is little reason to believe that installation of a thin BMD system will set it off and some reason to believe it might damp it. If the United States and the Soviet Union would agree to install thin missile defense systems, including point defenses for offensive missiles, they might be able to agree, either explicitly or tacitly, to smaller offensive missile forces inasmuch as such thin defensive missile systems would maintain second-strike capabilities with smaller numbers of offensive missiles. This likely would introduce some compensating economies in long-term defense costs by reducing the numbers of obsolescent missiles that would have to be replaced. However, MIRV will complicate but not invalidate the relevant calculations. Yet it is important to understand that a thin missile defense system may ease the problem of arms control. It is also important to understand that the budget for offensive and defensive strategic systems decreased from roughly $11 billion in 1962 to a projected $8 billion for 1970 (although not in a regular progression) despite inflation, a significant if implicit comment on the arms race.

The suggestion in 1968 by some in Washington that a "thin thin" BMD system would have advantages over the proposed "thin" Sentinel system are interesting. According to this argument, a "thin thin" system of approximately 100 missiles, as contrasted with the approximately 700 missiles of the rejected Sentinel system, would be adequate against a Chinese-type system if the United States struck first against the slow-reacting Chinese liquid-fuelled missiles upon warning that they were being readied for attack. The Chinese missiles that were unscathed in our first strike could then be shot down by the "thin thin" system. This system would be less effective against the Russians. On the other hand, it is argued, if the Russians were to extend their present BMD system to the equivalent of the proposed American thin systems, they would perforce install radar that would be sufficient to equip a "thick" system. If they were then to build additional defense missiles secretly, they could deploy them quickly in a crisis and acquire a first strike capability against us. This argument has some plausibility. However, it would commit us to a first strike against China that we might not be willing to implement for moral, strategic, or political reasons. Our information concerning the Chinese countdown might be mistaken; our intelligence might be defective; or the Chinese strike might be intended against Russia. Moreover, the Russians might stockpile their radars as well as their missiles. Installation of the complete system could not be made rapidly; however, the Russians might develop techniques permitting relatively rapid installation of the complicated electronics. Moreover, a decision for a "thin thin" system might delay seriously an

American decision to go into a thicker system if we discovered the Russians had deceived us.

It is not true that all proposed "thin" BMD systems have in their specifications the radar installations required for a "thick" system, although a BMD system that has the performance characteristics described earlier would have such specifications. However, this proposition is now unimportant. According to the *New York Times* of 24 April 1970, the Pentagon has observed work on Russian radar installations equivalent to those called for by the full Safeguard system and sufficient for a thick BMD system. The Soviets are thus three or four years ahead of us, even if the Senate permits the Administration to proceed.

BMD has one other interesting advantage. By increasing the United States defense capabilities against a small or unauthorized attack and by reducing the casualties that would be suffered in the unlikely event of a large nuclear interchange, BMD increases America's deterrent capabilities against attacks upon Europe. This improves the value of America's nuclear pledge, although I still would not place very great weight upon it, and reduces the political strain on NATO and the incentives for nuclear proliferation.[1]

The March, 1969, hearings on ballistic missile defense would be hilarious were they not so serious. An eminent scientist, Dr. Herbert York, argued that installation of a BMD system would delegate firing decisions that would have to be made within a few minutes to a stupid computer with input recognition problems and to a junior officer, thus taking nuclear decisions out of presidential hands. Even if such an event occurs, it is hardly likely to be an event that would increase the probability of war or of any other disastrous or nearly disastrous consequence. It might cause some diplomatic difficulties with the country over which the BMD warhead exploded, particularly if the case was one of a false alarm. Whether this event could occur at all depends upon firing doctrine. If one desires it, although it is difficult to see why one would, the system can operate under a firing doctrine in which no decisions in any circumstances can be made below presidential level; alternatively, one could have a doctrine in which no decision to launch can be made without presidential approval unless the radar indicates so large an attack that mistaken recognition possibilities can properly be ignored. The decision can still be made at a very high level of command, if one wishes. One would not want to burst a defensive missile over Canada without Canadian agreement in principle. Presumably the Canadians would not object to defensive measures against large-scale attack; if the attack were large enough, we might possibly ignore any prior agreement we have with them. Some might not wish to act even in accord with an agreement in the case of a possible small attack if the international situation seems very calm, as there is a remote but finite possibility of some retinal burn. There were, after all, two occasions on which SAC was not launched despite SAC standard operating procedures to the contrary. The price one pays for this kind of firing doctrine is that the BMD system is less good, under some circumstances, against accidental or unauthorized attacks. A city might go up in smoke unnecessarily. This would lead to many dead and perhaps to retaliation or war. Presumably the system would be good against limited retaliatory attacks, for these would occur in a time of war, during which time the firing doctrine presumably would be suitably altered. It is obvious that firing doctrine is a very sensitive matter and that it would need to remain classified.

Another alternative is to have a somewhat "thicker" system in which only short-range Sprints would be used against small intrusions. This would permit radar tracking into the atmosphere, thus virtually eliminating the possibility of a mistake. The probability of successful penetrations would be higher, however, and costs would be greater.

However, Dr. York's argument is quite misleading even apart from the previous points. He calls attention only to some possible costs of having a BMD system. He ignores the costs of not having such a system. Suppose radar indicates the possibility of attack. The president might now be faced with an agonizing choice. If he delays response, our strategic system may be seriously degraded. If he does not delay, his counterstrike against the apparent source of the attack may insure large-scale nuclear war. Would it not be better to have a BMD system that could degrade the attack or that perhaps might entirely forestall it? Would not the additional time for fact-finding, decisions, and perhaps negotiations be desirable under most circumstances? Moreover, would not the lives saved by such a system be worth something?

The old herring of an "inexorable" arms race was resurrected by Dr. George Kistiakowski. BMD, however, is compatible with a damped arms race. The genuine spur to an arms race is MIRV, which somehow does not seem to be at the heart of controversy and which can hardly be guarded against, short of "screw-driver-type" inspection.[2] It is very interesting that the Soviet Union, which has installed an apparently "thin" BMD system covering European Russia and directed against an American attack, has discovered that Safeguard will hinder arms talks only after repeated declarations to this effect by Senator Fulbright and others.

Before Russia had been told it would not negotiate if ballistic missile defense was installed, it had strongly urged such talks despite McNamara's decision to install Sentinel. Indeed, the Soviet Union specifically stated in 1967 at the eighteen-nation Disarmament Committee in Geneva that the decision to deploy Sentinel would not harm prospects for the nonproliferation agreement despite the fact that America's allies were then attacking the decision as a barrier to the treaty and to arms control. Even after the *Izvestia* article, *Pravda* took special note of Mr. Nixon's statement that his revised BMD proposal was not incompatible with arms control negotiations.

It is worth noting that a failure to begin BMD installations now might promote a strong and difficult-to-control arms race. The projected Russian first strike capability (discussed below) would be completed in 1974. The Safeguard system will be completed by then only if installation is begun soon. If this is not done and if the Russians do not slow down the installations of SS 9's, the only short-term counter for the United States will result in the rapid expansion of its offensive missiles. Thus the quantitative race will accelerate. Economies of operation will then likely force both sides to install MIRV; this will exacerbate the instabilities of the arms race and give the Russians a one-sided first strike capability because of the low yield of Minuteman III. This is not inevitable perhaps; but it is worth considering when arms race arguments are made against BMD.

Mr. Nixon's compromise proposal for protection of offensive missile bases only was perhaps the best that could be got in the political climate created by the sustained but irresponsible attacks by scientists on BMD. His proposal does provide added protection for our offensive missile forces now that the electro-magnetic pulse problem mentioned by Senator Goldwater in the 1964 campaign has probably been overcome. Mr. Nixon's proposal provides less protection against a Chinese attack or against an unauthorized or accidental attack against cities. These are low probability events, although hardly so low that they can be entirely discounted. It is difficult to see how reduced protection for our cities can satisfy anyone except those advocates of finite deterrence who perhaps fear that an American president will want to initiate a nuclear war except in that case in which the maximum number of Americans are held hostage to enemy attack. This chain of reasoning is reminiscent of the debate over shelters and has much of the same pathological quality. Increased protection of civilians will increase neither the Russian nor the American impetus to nuclear war. Neither country will lightly risk destruction of its large cities. Neither country will likely invest large sums of money for increased offense, unless this can produce a first strike capability, in the belief that additional deterrence is necessary. BMD has a possible marginal effect on the American willingness to come to the aid of Europe in case of Soviet attack. However, this effect is not so great that it is remotely likely to spur large Soviet expenditures to overcome it unless the Soviet Union has a definite plan to attack Western Europe. Fortunately, the controversy allowed Mr. Nixon to improve the radar placements of the BMD system—a design problem in Sentinel that would have made for blind spots for attacks from the South.

Secretary of State Rogers has stated during the Senate BMD hearings that the Nixon administration could "get out of it very quickly" if the Soviets "indicate that they want to get out of the defensive missile business." Even the usually sober Max Frankel of the *New York Times* accepted the assessment by the Senate Foreign Relations Committee that he thus "undercut all the administration arguments that Soviet offensive power, Communist China's missile program and the danger of accident made it essential to build a missile defense system now.[3] This statement is incorrect with respect to strategic problems and tells more about the state of hysteria that has been generated in Washington than about sound defense considerations. No one knows what is essential. We can only talk about risks, costs, and possible gains. If the Nixon administration agrees with the Soviet Union not to permit BMD systems, it avoids the dangers of a situation in which the Soviet Union has such a system and we do not—a situation that may exist today. Every study of the problem, including the figures in McNamara's 1968 posture statement—and those do not overstate the effectiveness of BMD—supports this conclusion.

Thus it is false to assert that this apparent concession undercuts the arguments for BMD with respect to the Russian missile build-up; and, despite McNamara's 1968 posture statement, this has always been the primary justification of the system. Nonetheless, there would be some very real costs to such a decision. These would include the lack of a defense against smaller nuclear powers and against accidental or unauthorized attacks. The United States and the Soviet Union would suffer a joint cost if one accepts the argument, as I do, that both sides would have better-protected second strike forces if both had BMD. Perhaps these factors led the Nixon administration to retreat from Mr. Rogers' statement. They may also have taken into account the inadvisability of failing to hedge against possible defects in land-based and Polaris missiles or improvements in Russian defensive measures. It is difficult to quarrel with a military "hedge" when it is cost-effective.

Secretary of Defense Laird has been accused of attempting

to create a missile gap theory as phony as the one of 1960 is believed to be. In the form in which the missile gap was propagandized in 1960 by John Kennedy and his liberal defense advisers, including Jerome Wiesner, there is some merit to the charge. No one knew that there was or would be a missile gap. The Soviet Union had the capacity to build enough missiles to knock out SAC. The important question centered on whether they were building them and how great the risk was. Most defense analysts thought the risk was too high, although I did not know any who thought the likelihood was as high as one in two. We face a similar but not identical problem with respect to the mid-1970's. The Soviet Union may well be able to knock out almost the entire Minuteman force with the SS 9's alone (they have other ICBM's, of course) despite additional hardening if we do not develop BMD, even if the accuracy and the reliability of the Russian SS 9's are no greater than that of our Minuteman III force and if they continue their present rate of production and if they have only three five-megaton warheads apiece. (They might do even better sooner.) The rate of production is subject to Russian decision. The other estimates are extremely conservative and almost surely understate the risk. Poseidon will remain as a retaliatory threat. But that force is expensive; its command and control is subject to possible defeat unless we adopt the incredibly dangerous firing doctrine of allowing individual ship commanders to fire at Russian cities whenever their communications are blacked out; and it is vulnerable to blackmail as the only surviving force element. Moreover, it is a serious mistake to allow an important element of our strategic force, such as Minuteman, to develop known vulnerabilities. Our bombers are known to be vulnerable to a first strike. If Minuteman also becomes vulnerable, then we may find ourselves at the mercy of vulnerabilities to our submarine fleet that we do not know about but that the Soviet Union does.

During the hearings in 1969, Dr. York was arguing, as was Dr. Rathjens, that Secretary Laird's projections did not make sense. However, Mr. Laird's estimates concerning the vulnerability of Minuteman were in fact so convincing that Dr. York soon held a press conference to argue that Minuteman was obsolete. Dr. Rathjens took more time but eventually switched arguments in the same manner. However, in the interim he had argued that Soviet missile accuracies would not be so good as Secretary Laird or even he had projected until it was pointed out that if he corrected for his misreading of a Pentagon chart on missile hardening, his calculations would have supported the case for BMD unless he then changed his assumptions concerning Soviet missile accuracies to fit his previous conclusions.

Dr. York's conclusion was excessive; most experts do not expect Soviet accuracies to be as great as Dr. York now projects until the late 1970's at best, and more likely not until the 1980's. Moreover, BMD is our best hedge against this, particularly given the possible vulnerabilities of SAC and Polaris. In any event, the situation is serious indeed, and possibly casts into doubt hypotheses by critics concerning Russian motivations.

Although some like to argue that the current Soviet missile build-up is a belated response to our 1961 build-up, there is no substantial evidence to support this position. There are other hypotheses that can be believed. One of these is that it was McNamara's announced policy of parity that encouraged the Soviet Union to believe that it could achieve a not incredible first strike capacity. Another is that the Soviet decision to build up its nuclear forces was unrelated either to the 1961 build-up or to the parity decision, but that it reflected instead a deliberate Soviet decision to avoid large defense expenditures until Russia was ready with its second- and third-generation systems. I do not believe that prudence justifies complacency in this situation, and it surely does not justify the dogmatic beliefs of the Senate liberals.

Although some aspects of military matters lend themselves to precise calculation in a manner quite different from political projections, many of the questions that deal with the application of strategic theory or strategic weapons do rest on speculations, informed judgments, analogies, and metaphors. Yet responsible political leaders cannot afford to leave them out of account, for the circumstances anticipated are, if unlikely, not of negligible probability. Moreover, the degree to which one guards against them may influence the probability with which they occur. Although there is no one-to-one relationship between one's political will and military preparedness, there is reason to believe that some sort of positive relationship does exist.

Political leaders and defense planners have to take into account both the actual costs of current military build-ups and the potential costs of a failure to incur current costs. Some current expenditures will turn out to be wasted. Either the threat guarded against will not materialize or the system will quickly become obsolete. This will introduce very difficult problems for defense cost analysis. However, the failure to pay costs now can lead in some cases to the generation of crises that would not otherwise have occurred or to the necessity for a larger later expenditure that could have been minimized by a smaller but earlier expenditure. Not one of the generalizations in this section sufficiently supports either a particular increase or a particular decrease in military expenditures; but the framework of discussion does provide a useful corrective for some discussions of this issue.

Notes

1. The American nuclear pledge has been reduced to a virtual nullity by the Senate debate on the nuclear nonproliferation treaty, in which Senator Fulbright agreed that the pledge established no new commitments.
2. Soviet testing of a MIRV-type system possibly could be detected. We would not be able to tell, however, whether they had installed it or how many they had installed, even in this case.
3. *New York Times* (March 28, 1969).

7   The American Role
in the World

Even though we are attempting to provide only perspectives
for policy in this book, the discussion would not have focus
without some consideration of particular substantive problems.
How should the United Nations be used by the United States?
Should the United States favor a united Europe? What is the
relationship of NATO to such objectives? How do projections
for the Soviet bloc fit into such goals? What should American
perspective be toward China and Japan? To what extent is
the United States in a position to influence change in the Third
World? Is there any validity in the attacks by critics on American interventionism? Does the United States have a special
mission in the world?

Although we can provide only perspectives for some aspects
of these problems, these perspectives can provide an orientation
for further analysis and investigation by the reader.

The United States and the United Nations

If the nation-state still plays a major role in the implementation of desired national and international values, what is the
appropriate role of the United Nations? If the United Nations
has a genuine, even if not a leading, role to play in the development of world order, it follows that those who desire to enhance
that role ought to be willing to incur some costs in order to
re-enforce it. The United Nations should be treated neither as
a mere instrument of American foreign policy, to be used for
motives of the moment, nor as a symbol of world democracy in
a world in which neither appropriate consensus nor adequate
representational techniques exist.

There was a tendency in the Truman administration to use the United Nations merely as an instrument of America's momentary policies; in the Eisenhower administration there was a tendency to use that organization as a surrogate for American policy making. The American effort under the Kennedy and Johnson administrations to use the nonpayment of dues by the Soviet Union as an instrument of policy also misused the organization. If the Soviet Union appropriately would not completely subordinate its national policy to the decisions of the organization—decisions that in many cases were contrary to important Russian interests and that had been maneuvered to passage by heavy American pressures in ways that were responsive to American interests—it hardly seems reasonable to have expected the Russians to pay to support such activities. Indeed, one wonders why the United States was not concerned with the precedent it was setting? The most appalling thing about the activity, however, was its clumsiness; what would have been gained by expulsion of the Russians from the United Nations? And what led the American representatives to think that they could talk the nations of the General Assembly into making such an expulsion or that they could make the threat credible in a way that would lead to Russian payment of dues against clearly contrary Russian interests?

Another American policy regarding the United Nations is one of involving it in disputes that can better be handled unilaterally. This goes along with an effort, even outside of the United Nations, to provide multilateral backing for American policies. No doubt on many occasions this can be useful, but often this policy seems based on naive, moralistic notions or on the effort to show Congress and the public that others are helping to bear the costs. In the case of Korea, the involvement of the United Nations made it easier to shift our objective from the original one of restoring the status quo ante to that of implementing the United Nations objective of unifying Korea. Since most events are overdetermined, perhaps this extension of objective would have happened anyway. But if the United Nations—supposedly a universal organization representing the entire world—had not been involved in the Korean War, it would not later have been forced to negotiate as an equal party with a China that it had condemned as an aggressor. Can an experience for the United Nations more humiliating than that easily be imagined?

In the case of Korea, only the United States had the military power to intervene effectively; despite the use of a United Nations flag, the effective military decisions were being made in Washington. Although the argument was made, perhaps not entirely illegitimately, that if the United Nations did not intervene, it would go the way of the League of Nations, it is difficult to see how a purely American venture would have served as a bad example. Moreover, in many other cases multilateral approaches are more likely to interfere with effective policy making or to result in the use of American resources for purposes contrary to American interests than they are to temper American mistakes or provide a framework more acceptable to opinion in the Third World. Although *ad hoc* multilateral activities have had some temporary successes, for example, in the Middle East, and although they perhaps can be useful in the future, they carry with them the costs and dangers, including that of ineffectiveness, for which the Middle East also serves as an example.

A typical Madison Avenue type of poster used to be shown in which there was a nuclear mushroom explosion with the caption "This or the United Nations." These obviously are not the alternatives; the United Nations is not the major agency for keeping the peace, although it is useful in the settlement of some disputes or in the moderation of minor quarrels. Overestimation of the organization will set it tasks it is ill-equipped to carry out and will likely lead to a form of disillusionment that will be harmful to the organization. On the other hand, merely using the organization as a momentary instrument of policy is likely to be inconsistent with its development or with its utilization for those modest purposes that under current conditions of international politics it is equipped to handle. The organization narrowly escaped disaster in the Congo; the big powers should be wary of forcing upon the organization burdens involving important conflicts of interest among the major powers that the organization has neither the managerial skills nor the information to deal with adequately.

The organization's mediatory and conciliatory aspects, however, would be strengthened by the acquisition of administrative responsibilities in areas not currently the focus of major rivalries. If, for instance, the United Nations were given the responsibility for securing access for all nations to the resources of the seas before the technology for exploitation of these resources has been developed, this supervisory function might be accepted by all nations at a time when they have no immediate, definite, and pressing contrary interests and might remain acceptable, even after the appropriate technology develops, to the extent that the uncertainties continue to outweigh the competitive advantages of disrupting the regime for control of the sea.

Such successful administrative activities might lead to similar activities in space. Even if these activities do not functionally expand and diversify, their success as a symbol of international management would probably help foster a climate of belief in which other problems become more tractable. The visibility of a minimum degree of order in the world might possibly, although not necessarily, have considerable influence on the perspectives of national leaders. In this respect, although the United Nations is not the alternative to mushroom clouds, it may become a not unimportant instrument for the maintenance of a reasonable minimum level of order and law in the world.

Europe and the United States

The most fateful questions of American statecraft concern the role of Europe in the world. For a generation American policy has been directed toward encouraging the unification of Europe in some form, even though a unified Europe would in many ways be able to compete much more successfully with the United States than does present-day Europe. Our policies have not been completely consistent, for one of the motives underlying our support for the nuclear nonproliferation treaty probably is a desire for a condominium with the Soviet Union, at least with respect to the nuclear issue. Our policies have never been completely articulated and their inconsistencies have never been removed.

The arguments for European unification are quite strong. The nation-state in Europe no longer serves as a sufficient focus for loyalty, despite de Gaulle's arguments to the contrary; there has been a noteworthy devolution of loyalty within the nation toward long-suppressed regional groupings, which perhaps could be better assimilated within a larger Europe than within existing national actors. In addition, with the change in the scale of economic activity, the European nation-state is not large or powerful enough to contain or to control economic organizations that can compete with their counterparts in the United States. Nor can Europe, as either a cultural or a political entity, exercise a role on the world scene in any way comparable to that of the United States as long as its influence is divided among a number of competing components. For the next decade at least, it appears unlikely that any single European nation can afford a stable and effective nuclear force; the setbacks to the French *force de frappé* as a consequence of the latest French troubles is, one would think, highly instructive in this respect. A united Europe would provide an alternative to German reunification and a framework within which eventual reunification might occur in a way less threatening to a number of important European and world interests.

If America ever retreats from Europe or if a change in the nuclear "balance" or in the American will to honor its nuclear protection of Europe is ever significantly reduced, the susceptibility of a disunited Europe to pressures from the Soviet Union might increase in a way threatening to United States security. Although the appropriate metaphor for the danger to Europe since 1945 has been that of the Czechoslovak coup of 1948 rather than that of an armed invasion out of the blue, the Soviet invasion of Czechoslovakia in 1968 serves as an example that the latter type of metaphor cannot entirely be ruled out of account. Although the explanation the Soviet Union eventually came up with, and that it has since stressed to the United States, is that it will not permit changes in the membership of the Soviet commonwealth, changes in explanations and rationales can occur coordinately with changes in the world situation. Indeed, the Soviet Union had earlier stressed national sovereignty more than had the United States. Moreover, if the growth of Soviet influence in Europe were to lead to increases in Communist influence in countries such as France and Italy, for instance, then conceivably the mantle of a Soviet socialist commonwealth could be extended to these countries by interpretation.

None of these possibilities should be regarded as now intended by the Soviet Union, although perhaps even this possibility cannot be excluded; yet the nature of the threat to the United States is so significant, even if only potential, that alternatives that reduce its likelihood are surely desirable.

The alternative of a united Europe met a significant barrier in the grand design of Charles de Gaulle that is only partly being lowered by President Pompidou. Only an intemperate writer would dare to deny the genius of de Gaulle; only a genius could be as grandly wrong as de Gaulle. Yet perhaps his abilities have been overestimated by some. The impeding of progress toward European unity and the reduction of the French commitment to NATO are negative or blocking measures rather than constructive measures. It is easier to be a wrecker than a builder. De Gaulle has been a consummate wrecker. He may even have permanently frustrated the movement toward European unity, for the motivations of European youth that were at one time being directed toward the ideal of a united Europe are now being turned toward more nationalistic or subnationalistic goals. This seems particularly the case in West Germany.

Nonetheless, even under former President de Gaulle, French elections showed a larger reservoir of support for European unity than many had thought likely. The French need for aid from other European countries during the crisis over the franc in 1968 demonstrated the vulnerability of the isolated French economy; and the political turmoil in the universities showed a possible, if unlikely, vulnerability of the political structure.

De Gaulle's view of the world, and his concordant policy prescriptions, seem, however, monumentally wrong. Apart from the problem of nuclear weapons, the conventional military vulnerability of the individual Western European countries is evident beyond question in an age of modern tanks and fast jets and massive Soviet forces. By massive applications of will de Gaulle almost managed to impose a nineteenth-century political structure upon Europe; but this structure is inadequate to the modern age and vulnerable to Soviet pressures. The French leadership that could have been achieved in the 1950's or 1960's for a united Europe, with a capital in Paris, is now replaced by West German predominance and the recognition and acceptance of this predominance by the West Germans. President de Gaulle's attempt to fend off England from Europe, as a possible base for American influence, could possibly have led to a permanent, and perhaps organic, American presence in England off the shores of France—a prospect less likely under Pompidou.

Alternative Soviet Possibilities

We cannot be sure what the alternatives are in the Soviet sphere. The Soviet Union's move in Czechoslovakia may have been a last grasp after imperial control. Or it may represent a reinvigoration of the Soviet Union under younger and more determined leadership. It may represent tighter and more permanent control over the satellites. It may foreshadow an extension of control to Rumania and Yugoslavia. It could even lead to membership in the Soviet Union by the Eastern European states. There were some possible indications that Walter Ulbricht in East Germany was attempting to move in this direction and there is even a remote possibility that in a regime and bloc crisis Soviet leaders might grasp at a temporary solution based on a Soviet empire extending from Vladivostok to the borders between the Germanies. Such an empire eventually might come under the control of an efficient and ruthless East German leadership, a possibility that Soviet leaders would be aware of but that they might risk under crisis conditions.

If we ever passively permit a Russian attack on Chinese nuclear facilities, perhaps from fear of Chinese radicalism or from a desire to protect the prospects for the nuclear nonproliferation treaty, we might open a Pandora's box. The Russians might then maintain tight control of their bloc through fear and they might find a pliable Chinese leadership that recognizes its dependence on Soviet aid, at least for a generation. Alternatively, they might have to maintain control by military force and by repression or risk isolation. They might then be forced into ever riskier ventures to maintain their rule.

There are still many other alternatives we have not discussed. Some of those already mentioned may seem wildly implausible to some because they diverge so much from the patterns we think we see emerging. Yet we overestimate the predictability of these matters if we dismiss such possibilities too lightly. If either of the last two possibilities were to become manifest, even a united Europe might not be independently viable. However, it is still premature to anticipate and to plan for this possibility. Although we want, if possible, to avoid measures that would preclude later attempts to compensate for them, these latter possibilities are much too speculative to serve as a focus for meaningful political activities at the present time. Moreover, attempts now to meet these contingencies would perhaps interfere with efforts to cope with more likely problems. Yet, although one cannot preclude the possibility that the international system will continue as it is, it is inadequate to assume that it will do so.

Things might have gone in a more favorable direction in the past and might do so again in the future. If the Soviet Union had allowed Czechoslovakia to go its own way, then, whatever the intellectual inadequacies and imprudent strategical calculations that were part of the détente psychology, the Soviet Union might have retreated within its own lair and might have moderated its internal policies; détente, albeit accompanied by other dangers resulting from the Balkanization of Europe, might then have permitted a retreat in American responsibilities and a relaxation of American efforts to support European unification. For the present at least it seems unrealistic to assume that we can return to where we were before the Soviet invasion of Czechoslovakia, that we can follow the policies that then seemed appropriate, at least to some, and that we can relax our efforts. We cannot ignore the possibility that it was the relaxation of American efforts to maintain military superiority, that it was the clear American unwillingness to be seriously concerned with the fate of Czechoslovakia and the damage that de Gaulle had done to NATO and to European unity, that provided the context within which the risks of the Soviet attack on Czechoslovakia became minimal.

The Soviet leadership has usually been quite cautious, but its success in this instance, if it is consolidated, might possibly at some later date moderate its cautiousness. If it is unwise and too great an extrapolation from the evidence to assume that the Soviet effort in Czechoslovakia was anything other than an extremely limited effort or that it was one which, after success, they now desire to expand, we cannot ignore the possibility that our continuing reactions to their behavior will affect their future expectations concerning the risks and possible advantages of alternative policies.

NATO, the Soviet Union, and Europe

The bridge between a potential European response to Soviet power and an Atlantic union is to be found in NATO. The problems involved in the conventional defense of Europe posed by recent French policy are extremely complex and cannot be discussed here. One can only hope that the Pompidou government reverses de Gaulle's policy. On the other hand, it would be a mistake to assume that de Gaulle's position is unique in France. After the London meeting of the foreign ministers in 1947, then Foreign Minister Bidault of France attempted to explain why France found herself in the camp of England and the United States after London rather than in the independent role she essayed at Moscow. Bidault offered to the Foreign Affairs Committee of the French parliament the explanation that events between the two meetings had caused an unbridgeable rupture between the Soviet Union on one hand and England and the United States on the other. It is significant that the first cause assigned by Bidault for the unbridgeable rupture between the two camps was the Marshall Plan, whereas the Truman Doctrine was not mentioned. This appears to have been a "Freudian" slip by M. Bidault. The Marshall Plan was not as potential an instrument in the Cold War as was the Truman Doctrine, but it may better explain France's decision. If the wartime alliance could not hold together to control Germany, France had to protect herself.

This is, in fact, the explanation given by M. Bidault. Although he finds the individual needs of the parties sufficient to explain their failure to reach agreement on Germany, he does not believe they explain the breaking up of the conference itself. *"Tous ces désaccords partiels ne sont qu'un aspect des oppositions fundamentals qui séparent les Alliés. . . ."* France would refuse to regard this rupture as permanent, and when conditions arose permitting the reforging of allied unity on Germany, France would use its good offices to bring this event to pass. But *"(p)our le moment, il faut vivre."* Thus, it is not entirely unlikely that every time tensions diminish, a French government will seek to mute its differences with Moscow and to reduce its role in NATO.

At best, NATO is presently a reserve instrument of policy, rather than something that can be counted on as continuously viable. The American strategic nuclear force will serve to deter the Russians under most usual and many unusual circumstances, despite de Gaulle's claims to the contrary. However, there are a number of circumstances that European statesmen cannot dismiss from their calculations under which the Russians may be able to deter us from intervening, particularly if they achieve some degree of nuclear superiority. It would be an act of constructive statesmanship for the United States to encourage and to offer to support with "know how" the development of a European nuclear force that could be used under either of two circumstances: a nuclear attack by the Soviet Union or a massive incursion of Soviet forces across a defined border and a failure to withdraw within a stated interval of time upon notice. Such a force would improve European morale during a crisis and would also make less likely the deliberate launching or escalation of a crisis by the Soviet Union. It would reduce the dangers arising from the presently unstable *force de frappé* possessed by France: dangers that would include self-deterrence for the French and the possibility of a Russian pre-emptive attack that might accidently involve the United States in an otherwise avoidable nuclear war.

If the European nations other than France agreed to form a European strategic nuclear force, there would be important pressures on the French to enter lest the Germans play an important role in a nuclear force that surpassed the French *force de frappé* in viability and effective striking power and over which the French had no control. Although such a joint European nuclear force would have even graver defects with respect to the defense, for instance, of Yugoslavia or Rumania than does the present American force with respect to its defined responsibilities in the NATO area, it nonetheless would serve to diminish the likelihood of a Soviet venture in areas close to important European interests. If it proves infeasible to establish such a force, then the next line of policy might be American support for independent national nuclear forces in Europe or alternatively a quick transfer capacity for use in a crisis.

To the extent that NATO serves either as a viable instrument in its own right or as a bridge to something eventually even more important, such as Atlantic Union, we will have to learn how to give our allies more effective roles in the organization and greater control over relevant strategic forces, at least insofar as they affect directly the European area. We do not necessarily want to increase veto powers, as in the ill-fated MLF example. But the policy decisions leading to implementation of strategic weaponry must recognize that NATO is a partnership, that even if the United States remains the leading nation it is no longer as completely dominant as it was in 1949 or 1951. The actual employment of nuclear weapons might be under the same conditions as proposed earlier for the European nuclear force.

Alternatively, a European nuclear force might be an essential ingredient for a united Europe—a development that might permit a meaningful European security treaty within the framework of which the United States could withdraw from Western Europe and the Soviet Union from Eastern Europe. Even if the latter consequence did not follow, such a development might defuse world politics by mitigating the confrontation between the United States and the Soviet Union. It might also immensely weaken the attraction of the Soviet Union for radicals in Western Europe by revealing even more clearly the reprehensible reasons for a continued Soviet presence in Western Europe. Such a development would involve risks as well as gains but they might be worthwhile. In any event, we cannot merely maintain existing structures of action that lack clear rationales and major support.

The advent of a Socialist government in Germany may possibly increase new trends in German foreign policy. The new regime may offer recognition of East Germany in exchange for guarantees concerning West Berlin. In any event, it is likely to continue the policy of Ostpolitik, although in ways less upsetting to the Soviet Union than in the past. It will likely sign the treaty on nuclear nonproliferation while attempting to influence its control provisions.

It cannot be excluded that such a policy will gradually dissolve European barriers while permitting a retreat of both American and Soviet troops, thus ending the cold war. But some dangers are involved even if the Brandt administration pursues this policy slowly and flexibly. The United States may be sufficiently impressed by growing détente to withdraw its troops prematurely, particularly given its pressing financial concerns. In any event, Russian troops will remain closer by even if both sets of troops withdraw simultaneously.

The German signature of the nuclear nonproliferation treaty may reassure the Russians. On the other hand, the Russians have already hinted that the treaty will outlaw nuclear weapons potential as well as capability-in-being, although such an interpretation would not be imposed on "peaceful" states. The treaty would then constitute a form of Russian pressure on West Germany—the state that the treaty is directed against anyway in the Russian view, as they have made clear—if it did not pursue a policy accepted by the Russians as "peaceful." The treaty itself is based on an irrational criterion, namely, the date on which a state became nuclear. Thus, a West German signature on the treaty is likely in the long run to produce nationalistic rather than liberal reactions in Germany and to speed rather than to slow progress toward the acquisition of nuclear weapons, particularly if the American commitment has weakened in the meantime.

Alternatively, in an effort to avoid the new impasse, West Germany may deal directly with a Soviet Union which prefers an agreement even with a nationalist West Germany to the dangers of a confrontation, particularly given its China problem. The ultimate consequences of such a development are difficult to foresee but they would not likely prove reassuring.

Japan and China: Some Perspectives

The role of the major Asian nations, China and Japan, in the American perspective deserves much more serious attention than it can receive in these pages. Japan is now the second leading industrial power of the non-Communist world. Although virtually devoid of natural resources, Japan's phenomenal rate of economic growth indicates a vigor that must soon have its outlet in political influence. The Japanese are already beginning to extend themselves economically and politically in Southeast Asia and even to play an important role in the economic development of Russian Siberia. They have a greater capacity to develop a nuclear weapons system than does any single Western European nation. Eventually it will be inconsistent with their own security and their sense of dignity for them to remain dependent upon the United States for military protection, a protection that might not be available in some credible crises. It is important for

Japan and the United States to remain on friendly terms; the more smoothly the transition from Japanese dependence is arranged, the more likely it is that the relationship in the longer run will be friendly and useful. We should give Okinawa back to Japan and give up our bases there and in Japan proper. Despite their logistic importance, they are a great political embarrassment. They corrupt Japanese politics and divert Japanese perceptions from Japanese security problems. Japan will never face up to its role in the world while the American presence continues.

The problem of American relations with China will not likely be solved by immediate recognition or the seating of Communist China in the United Nations. It is absurd to argue that the existence of Communist China is a fact that the American government must recognize, for, in the Warsaw meetings, American officials have probably conducted more extensive negotiations with Communist China than has any non-Communist nation that has recognized Communist China. Immediate recognition would probably be regarded as a sign of weakness by China; it is dubious that China would accept United Nations membership except under conditions that would deliberately be made so onerous that they could not be accepted by the organization. The issues that divide the United States and China—American protection of the Nationalist government on Taiwan and American policy in Viet Nam—are not easily resolvable. In any event, hostility toward the United States probably serves internal domestic purposes in China too well to be dispensed with immediately.

Nonetheless certain straws in the wind that indicate the potentiality for improving relationships have recently occurred. The Chinese cleverly arranged for a resumption of the Warsaw discussions early in the Nixon administration; Chiang Ching-kuo, the heir-apparent to government leadership on Taiwan, has stated privately that the return to the mainland is a dream, a figment of the imagination. However, the problem of Taiwan, is a very difficult problem to solve, even if the Nationalists give up the dream of returning to the mainland, for the acquisition of Taiwan as part of China is a goal that no nationalistic Chinese government could easily forswear. Yet, given the obvious opposition of the population on Taiwan to Communist rule, the United States could not easily betray the guarantee of protection it has offered the twelve million people on Taiwan.

China is concerned about the clashes with Russian troops on their mutual border. Fear that this would occur was another possible motive for the Chinese decision to improve relations with the United States by recommencing the Warsaw talks. In any event, despite the very difficult specific conflicts of interest between China and the United States, China's more direct conflicts of interest lie with the Soviet Union. China, moreover, is useful to the United States at least in part in diverting Soviet attention from Europe.

Although one cannot exclude the possibility that a developed China—and such a China is not on the near horizon—will reverse its present conservative foreign policy and become a direct menace to important American interests, those interests are still less important than the ones Russia menaces. It is difficult to see how even a tacit American-Russian front against China would benefit the United States. Despite the potential concordances of interest between China and the United States, the United States has a distinct interest in a strong Japan that would serve as a bulwark against China if the latter developed excessive ambitions in Asia.

Nuclear Proliferation

The nuclear nonproliferation treaty represents one attempt to halt the spread of nuclear weapons. Although such an effort is desirable, it is doubtful that the particular means chosen will be effective and they may very well prove counter-productive. The distinction the treaty writes into law between nuclear and non-nuclear states—acquisition of weapons before the effective date of the treaty—is an irrational distinction from a legal standpoint. The dangers arising from this self-serving irrational distinction could be mitigated by nuclear disarmament. However, neither the Soviet Union nor the United States intends seriously to move toward nuclear disarmament and there are good reasons related to the instabilities arising from the process toward nuclear disarmament why they should not do so. The nuclear guarantees offered by the United States and the Soviet Union to denuclearized states are inherently incredible and, in any event, contain effective escape mechanisms.

The treaty, in effect, is designed to establish a Soviet-American condominium, at least in the field of strategic weapons. Such a condominium rests on no defensible ground and effectively relegates other major nations to client status. Such a relegation is politically immoral and also will likely prove ineffective. It may well create the kinds of resentments that accelerate rather than decelerate the nuclear arms race.

The nuclear nonproliferation treaty is intended to operate primarily against the Germans by the Russians. It thus makes a doubly invidious distinction in that case. It is unlikely that new generations of Germans—it is more than twenty-five years since the war—will find palatable a permanent attribution of guilt.

By forgoing a serious effort to create a European nuclear force, the United States declined to sponsor a distinction that might have decelerated the spread of nuclear weapons: a distinction between those groupings that could afford adequate command and control and reasonable research and development and those that could not, a distinction grounded in practicalities rather than in law. By ineffectively opposing a French force, the United States encouraged the strategically invalid notion that an effective nuclear force could be developed by an independent moderate-sized nation against great-power resistance. By sponsoring the nuclear nonproliferation treaty, the United States increases the likelihood of a Soviet pre-emptive strike against China based on a self-serving treaty interpretation—an outcome that, although not highly probable, could have incalculable consequences if it occurs. One can only hope that these considerations are invalidated with the passage of time. None-

theless, the nuclear nonproliferation treaty is another instance
of the truism that good intentions do not make good politics.

Perspectives on the Third World

The problems of the third areas of the world are so complex
that the few cursory remarks possible here cannot provide even
the framework of a useful perspective. Yet some things might
perhaps be said. It is asserted by many critics that Viet Nam
is an example that proves that the United States is incapable of
fighting counterguerrilla wars, that it must fail in such wars
because it lacks the knowledge and because its administrative
apparatus is too clumsy to succeed. It is doubtful that American
difficulties in Viet Nam have demonstrated anything of the
sort. Much more difficult tasks were undertaken when the
Western allies attempted the task of constructing a democratic
government in western Germany and when the United States
attempted alone to accomplish a similar venture in Japan.

It is one thing to install Communism in a country with the
aid of the Red Army and a local Communist Party; for a
democratic country to move in as an occupying power and to
attempt to restructure the entire political life of a nation is on
the face of it absurd. Even further absurdities and intellectual
stupidities can be found in the way the job was handled. For
instance, in Japan the American occupation authorities arrested
nearly all nonextreme labor union leaders and newspaper editors,
so that the labor unions and the editorial pages were dominated
during and immediately after the occupation period by Communists or by even more radical Socialists. Yet in both nations
reasonably viable democratic regimes exist and both countries
are remarkable examples of economic progress.

The United States has done badly in Viet Nam; but under
other circumstances or under different direction it might have
done much better. An earlier and less gradual escalation and
an earlier movement toward political reform might have dis-
couraged North Vietnamese intervention and might have undercut the basis of rebellion. Despite American errors, the Viet

Cong are not ten feet tall either. Apparently they made serious military mistakes, including the Tet offensive and subsequent military moves that depleted the Viet Cong infrastructure.

It is possible that the Tet offensive had primarily political objectives and that some of these were achieved, including the psychological impact on the United States. There are many competent observers who believe that one of the reasons the North Vietnamese finally entered into negotiations is that they have been unable to continue to supply trained military cadres in sufficient numbers for operations in the south. There are also those who believe that the war might have been fought much more effectively with a different military strategy that emphasized not major sweeps and point defenses but instead small, systematic clearing-and-holding operations and mobile defenses in depth by popular forces. This writer is one of those who believes that the military strategy has been very bad; yet recent apparent successes by the American military indicate that the enemy is not doing so well either. For instance, during Tet the Viet Cong were unable to penetrate successfully 21 cities in which there were no American troops. Such local defense encouraged President Thieu to distribute large numbers of rifles to the population (a move he had previously feared), in the expectation that the rifles would now be used effectively against the Viet Cong.

Counterguerrilla and pacification measures have had much greater success than might have been predicted.[1] The new First Secretary of the North Vietnamese Communist Party, Le Duan, has warned that the war may "drag on."[2] There is reason to believe that a shortage of trained cadres, as mentioned earlier, and the difficulty of drafting able men are impeding the North Vietnamese in launching major attacks. Many responsible observers believe that, except for measures forced by American public opinion, the war would be in sight of victory.

In any event, despite the enormous cost of the Vietnamese war, even if the country is lost the venture has not been a total failure. Despite the ridicule directed at the domino metaphor and despite the fact that the individual problems of the other nations of the area are different from those of Viet Nam, and in some ways not quite so severe, the metaphor has distinct merit.

A failure to have intervened in Viet Nam likely would have had serious repercussions in the rest of Southeast Asia and perhaps also in India and Japan. Moreover, the fact that the United States has expended so much blood and resources in Viet Nam provides it with an opportunity to use that situation as a demonstration of its will to intervene. It is true that President Johnson's withdrawal from the 1968 presidential race under pressure on this issue obscures and perhaps countervails against this lesson. The fact, however, that both presidential candidates accepted American responsibilities maintains open the possibility of acting so that our losses will not have been in vain. Much depends upon how we conduct ourselves in the future. If the final outcome is favorable or at least not very unfavorable, or if there is a significant temporal gap between our withdrawal and an unfavorable outcome, we can conduct negotiations with other Asian states in a manner that is not destructive of our credibility. There are, however, ways in which we have at least the possibility of maintaining our credibility even if the outcome is unfavorable; for instance, by casting the blame, justly or unjustly, upon the inability of the South Vietnamese to organize successfully for their own defense, if we establish commitments and a military posture that are reassuring to other Southeast Asian nations. The eventual state of public opinion and the public posture of the Senate will play obvious roles here.

If the worst occurs, it may become necessary for the United States in its public declarations to blur its contribution to the failures in South Viet Nam. In this case it will be important not to forget that the United States allowed itself to play so large a role in South Viet Nam that the South Vietnamese depended upon us and neglected to carry through the measures that might otherwise have maintained the viability of their own regime.

One good feature of the clear determination of the American public to reduce its commitment in South Viet Nam is the effect it has had upon the South Vietnamese. In the author's opinion, it has always been a defect of American policy, one he has warned against privately in the past, that the United States has not presented the South Vietnamese government with a small but important bill of particulars that would constitute a requisite for the maintenance of American involvement in South Viet Nam. Also at fault until recently was the unwillingness of the United States adequately to recognize the important political, as opposed to the merely military, aspects of our activities. There were blind spots; for instance, it never occurred to the American government, at least in the sense of taking action, even after it had been called to its attention, that it would be cheap— compared with our military expenditures—to buy up land in certain areas where the landlords had particularly bad reputations, even if the landlords were given a ten or twenty percent premium on the value of their property. Despite all these mistakes, American involvement is not clearly a failure. Moreover, there is still an opportunity for a favorable outcome.

However, the overthrow of Prince Sihanouk in Cambodia has precipitated a perilous situation in that nation and has been accompanied by a new North Vietnamese drive in Laos that may threaten the position of Souvanna Phouma. The decision by President Nixon to permit South Vietnamese military operations in Cambodia was dangerous. Coming after the refusal of the Russians to sponsor a general conference for the former Indochina area and the Chinese decision to support Sihanouk in exile, and after a secret offer not to intervene in Cambodia if the North Vietnamese did not step up their activities in that nation, the Nixon administration apparently came to the conclusion that the North Vietnamese were now seeking to change the status quo in both Cambodia and Laos, that they were likely to succeed, and that this would constitute a clear major threat to the Vietnamization program in South Viet Nam. Also, in view of the willing cooperation of the Cambodian government, the limited offensive against the enclave possibly may give the Vietnamization policy an important six-months' respite. These estimates may be wrong, but it is unlikely that the administration would have intervened in the face of such vigorous bipartisan opposition in the Senate unless the evidence for it had appeared convincing. There are now many uncontrollable elements in the situation that defy prediction. The Nixon administration, confronted by extremely dangerous alternatives, may have committed hara kiri. Harassed by an irresponsible Senate, its position may have become untenable whatever it did. If, however, it is lucky as well as courageous, the decision to intervene was likely the one chance it had to preserve its Vietnamization program—short of precipitate retreat—in the circumstances in which it found itself. Much will now depend upon the Vietnamese. Perhaps this is as it should be. Moreover, whatever the merits of intervention in the first place, precipitous cutting and running likely would have the quasi-domino effects we speak of below.

It is difficult to apply generalizations to the third areas of the world. It is true, of course, that the United States does not have the resources or the administrative capacity to intervene everywhere. It is also true that we have intervened in some places unwisely. This writer would include the Congo in the list of places where the United States intervened unwisely, even though in this case, as things turned out, the intervention did not involve any serious costs and may even have produced some good. We did, however, misinterpret the meaning of Communism in that particular African context and act on the basis of extremely inadequate information.

This writer is not convinced, however, that Viet Nam was the wrong place for intervention. Marxist Communism does have meaning in the Asian context. Moreover, even if a Ho Chi Minh-dominated Viet Nam might have struggled for independence between China and Russia, it would not have been quite in the position of Yugoslavia's Tito.

Tito was forced to mute his revolutionary activities after his split with Stalin at least partly because of his dependence upon the West and partly because of his attempt to forge a quasi-alliance with other Mediterranean powers. Ho Chi Minh's maneuverability between Russia and China would in all likelihood have enabled him to force the two major Communist nations to compete in supplying him with the sinews for national liberation wars in the former Indochina, and in all probability eventually against Thailand and Malaysia. (There are ethnic affinities throughout the entire area that extend to Southwest China.) Moreover, had the United States not intervened in force, the likelihood that Indonesian officers would have had the assurance to oppose the attempted Communist coup likely would have been much lower. A strong Communist surge in Indochina and Southeast Asia would likely have had an impact on Japan and Australia. Combined with eventual Soviet activities in Eastern Europe and with the reduced credibility of the United States, this might have had a severe impact on the political future of the Western European nations.

Of course, these are speculations; things could have happened differently. Hard scientific evaluations are not possible here. But the assertion that South Viet Nam was not only not vital but not even important to the security of the United States begs a large number of questions. It reads large the costs imposed by the Vietnamese War and takes for granted the not improbable stabilizing consequences that the war has had elsewhere in Asia and Europe. The large European opposition to American involvement is merely a sign of American unpopularity; our position probably would have been much worse had we remained liked but discredited. No doubt the possible nightmares sketched here will be rejected as absurd speculations by those who preferred alternative policies; but at least these speculations sound a cautionary warning against glib and unsceptical assumptions concerning the consequences of an American failure to have intervened.

It may not be wholly without merit to note in this context that Senator Fulbright, who began by ridiculing the domino theory, now takes the position (April, 1970) that a victory of Communism in all of former Indochina, and perhaps elsewhere in Southeast Asia, will not threaten important American interests. If the Senator succeeds in advancing this result, perhaps he will then discover that Indonesia, Japan, and India are not really important either. And, although it is likely easier for the Senator to write off Asians or other colored peoples than Europeans, there is an inherent, if less than inevitable, logic in his position that has long been foreshadowed in the subtle but vital qualifications he has attached to the defense of Europe and that become manifest in his unfriendly attitudes toward Israel.

If things ever reach the pass where the defense of Western Europe is in question—and I hope and believe they will not—perhaps the Senator will then find the cause in American arrogance and advise us to march in step with developments elsewhere in the world. Of course, political life confounds disembodied logics, and I do not regard the developmental sequence sketched above as necessarily compelling. Yet the perspective I far prefer to that of the Senator's is one based on the recognition that we cannot insulate ourselves from political and moral value changes elsewhere in the world. It is not necessary that other nations copy American institutions or values. Yet if the balance of hostility to these institutions and values shifts dramatically, mere nuclear power—even if, contrary to the implications of the Senator's advice, we maintain adequate deterrence—will not protect those aspects of our cultural heritage that give meaning to survival.

One last brief point may be worth mention. I will not defend the incompetent way in which policy was justified by the Johnson administration. On the other hand, efforts by the opposition to cast doubt upon its explanations of policy suffered from serious simplisms. That the administration on one occasion would stress international Communism, on another external attack, and on still another an effort to aid the Vietnamese people by preventing a totalitarian takeover is not evidence for the proposition that the grounds are inconsistent or that some of the alleged motivations are false. It is rare in cases of statecraft that a single motivation appropriately accounts for a decision. The United States might be opposed to totalitarian regimes but not so opposed that it would pay the price of a Vietnamese war to prevent a takeover otherwise favorable to the United States. The United States might be favorable to opposing takeovers inimical to its international interests but not at the price of imposing through its efforts a harsh regime on a resisting population. The United States might be opposed to international aggression but unwilling to pay any significant cost to prevent it if the results of the aggression were otherwise favorable. These are threshold motivations. If the cost is low enough, any of them may suffice to induce action. As the cost rises, the size of the disvalued consideration must also rise or other considerations must come into play. Even this badly oversimplifies the process. Any decision involves potential gains and costs over a wide range of variables. It is rare—indeed it is unheard of—that any particular decision will be better than every other possible decision over the entire range of variables. Thus there will almost invariably be a list of reasons why a decision should be taken and a list why some alternative should be taken instead. Any systematic discussion—I have not attempted to produce one here and I have not seen one elsewhere—would attempt to compare alternative decisions across a wide range of variables.

Dangers of a Reactive Foreign Policy

Foreign policies are often reactions to past lessons or supposed lessons. Often the public and also statesmen react by changing policies that seemed to fail rather than by adjusting policies to new circumstances. Even those who consider our intervention in Viet Nam as in some sense a "disaster" should not entirely overlook the problems that were avoided by intervention. Depending upon circumstances, the transformation of the regimes of Southeast Asia into Communist regimes might have given rise—and this is not that unlikely—to a myth of "betrayal." Had such a myth developed, this might have led to a later intervention under more explosive and less controllable circumstances.

These remarks are speculative. However, consideration of one reactive sequence from the past might serve an appropriate cautionary note. For instance, the results of the appeasement process during the 1930's are well known, but there are some interesting aspects that are not so well understood. The usual explanation is that Hitler could easily have been stopped—or even overthrown—in the 1935-1938 period, but that British appeasement, particularly at Munich, only whetted his appetite, consolidated his support, and produced the war. The first half of this proposition is correct; but the second half, to the effect that appeasement produced the war, is somewhat misleading, for other intervening variables were necessary to produce war— at least at the time at which it occurred. The British actually stood up to Hitler during the first Czechoslovak crisis in the spring of 1938. The shock produced by their temerity then led, even if not directly and without qualification, to the capitulation at Munich. Disillusionment of the British public with appeasement followed its wholehearted support for the process. The March, 1939, occupation of the remainder of Czechoslovakia by Germany led to the ill-advised British rigid guarantee to Poland—a guarantee that constituted a blank check for Polish foreign policy. The guarantee to Poland virtually insured German involvement in the west if Germany went to war with Poland and thus minimized the possibility that the German armies would continue eastward against the Russians. Without such an assurance, the pact with the Nazis likely would have looked excessively menacing to Stalin. A direct border with the Germans in the absence of a German war with Britain and France probably would have been the last thing Stalin wanted. However, without the pact with Russia, Germany would have faced a major war on two fronts and, therefore, would not have been as likely to follow a policy leading to general war. Although the description offered here is an oversimplification and surely does not involve logical entailment, it does indicate the extent to which attempts by human beings to correct the errors or supposed errors of the past sometimes lead them into ever more compromising predicaments. We might do well to avoid the siren call of those who would like to reverse our policies or even to reverse or to correct in substantial ways our institutional processes in order to guard against the errors of the past.

The Critics, Policy Control, and Policy Perspectives

If critics of present American policy merely want to make the point that many interventions, whether political, economic, or cultural, have unanticipated consequences that may arise either from American ignorance of the area, from its lack of administrative skill, or from the absence of appropriate social or political theories, the point can be conceded freely. However, it must be noted that the failure to intervene also has many unanticipated consequences; and it is at least not clear that these are better.

Surely Americans should view their comparative ignorance with humility; they should refrain from seeking to impose provincial American values abroad; and they should not be misled into believing that democracy, as we understand it, can grow on any soil. Yet it is difficult to believe that very many important American decision makers hold such ideas in the form in which they are so actively combatted by the critics.

We do have human and political interests in intervention. There may be important countervailing interests as well, for instance, in the aforementioned case of Haiti. It would be sad indeed, however, if we viewed human poverty, ignorance, cruelty, and even malevolence elsewhere as no concern of ours. Even if democracy cannot find firm roots everywhere, there may still be useful distinctions between regimes, such as the South Vietnamese regime, that permit at least some opposition and that either permit or do not have the strength to put down local particularisms, and relatively totalitarian regimes, such as the Chinese regime, that have the organizational capacity and the will to uproot the culture of an entire people and to impose a regimented system upon them.

Surely the United States should not support every reactionary regime merely because it is anti-Communist or oppose every revolutionary change because it might lead to a Communist government. On the other hand, revolution is not inherently good. In Iran there is now a rapid degree of growth in the gross national product. Wealthy Iranians are beginning to reinvest their money in their own country rather than to export it to Switzerland. Neighboring Iraq, with its socialist revolution and its revolutionary ideology and with comparable oil wealth, is experiencing stagnation and misery. Even some revolutions that accomplish some good often do it at considerable human cost. The Castro regime in Cuba has provided temporary dignity for at least some of the lower classes but at enormous sacrifices to the dignity and freedom of other parts of the population, some of whom, including working-class types, blacks, and professionals, have braved machine-gun fire in an attempt to escape.

Perhaps some of the assertions of the critics are useful corrections to past generalizations or past policies. However, they go much too far; they are made with too little discrimination; and they assert as general what is surely only particular. Although some forms of intervention can and should be avoided, this writer believes that the world is becoming so closely interrelated that the United States with its huge political, economic, ideological, and social power cannot avoid affecting the destinies of people in the remotest parts of the world. It does so whether it intervenes or fails to intervene. Almost any decision it makes is in effect a form of intervention.

The distinction that can most usefully be made is that between wise and unwise intervention. This distinction cannot be a general one. It must rest on the facts of the particular case or at least upon reasonable interpretations as to what the facts are. It must be considered in light of the available alternatives. We are too much part of the world to withdraw. Even efforts to sanitize our intervention, as in suggestions that we provide aid multilaterally or through the United Nations, could conceivably have much worse consequences than unilateral American aid.

Perhaps the greatest problem is that it is very difficult to ask in the heat of an intense crisis the hard questions that need to be answered. Yet if the crisis is not intense, there is for that very reason a tendency to drift into incremental decisions through postponement. Efforts to engage in long-range planning usually fail both because immediate problems call upon the personnel working on the longer range problems and because the decisions made in the short term often make the longer range plans irrelevant.

These are hard problems; these are dilemmas of decision making; and there are no facile solutions for them. Mistakes are inevitable. Decisions press, and there is not enough time to consider any but the most central. The disturbances to the system overload the capacity for decision making. Efforts to tie the hands of the executive only make the process more cumbersome, more inefficient, more deadly. If the executive runs the risk of operating within an intellectual framework based on a set of fixed ideas and therefore needs criticism and the input of ideas from outside, the one thing it does not require is the further internal complication of the decision making process. It may need a slap in the face but it does not need its collective arm in a sling.

Naturally all critics, including this writer, believe they have better solutions for particular problems than does the government. Sometimes we are right. At a minimum, there ought to be effective channels for the communication of these opinions. Some critics, however, seem to feel a need to control the government. They appear not to recognize that others would like to control it from a different point of view. They complain that their advice is not being listened to; but it could be listened to only at the expense of someone else's advice. The president especially must feel a prisoner within a process that includes so many conflicting demands and so much in the way of conflicting advice.

This attempt to control the government manifests the same neurotic characteristic that the American government sometimes displays in attempting to control every minor situation abroad, even though it lacks appropriate information and administrative personnel. We must learn to control this impulse, both at the governmental and at the private organizational levels, unless we are to impede and eventually corrupt the decision making process in a way that will be destructive of American values. Foreign policy protests seem to be a curious equivalent of adolescent rebellion; although sometimes there is genuine ground for complaint, the results are rarely salutary.

The suggestions made by the Senate Foreign Relations Committee for control of American foreign policy are peculiarly unresponsive to the nature of the world in which we live. Senator Fulbright complains that American involvement in Laos was never submitted to the United States Senate for approval. But such submission would have been inconsistent with the objectives of the intervention. It is the informal character of the intervention that allows other states not to overreact. For instance, in the Korean War, the Chinese troops were officially classed as "volunteers," although they were in organized Chinese divisions. This fiction allowed the United States to avoid a direct war with China on the Chinese mainland and served valid purposes of both sides. Similar fictions may provide a major barrier to a nuclear escalation in some future crisis or, alternatively, to a severe defeat of American interests.

Senator Fulbright distrusts executive control of foreign policy. His suggested reforms, however, would hobble policy. They would delay interventions until the situation had deteriorated and until enemy states had so overcommitted themselves that direct confrontations would be difficult to avoid. Although he has argued that the administration had no right to go to war in Vietnam without Senatorial consent, would he have preferred a declaration of war with its implications for dissent and for military escalation? Does he desire to force us to choose in every case between nonintervention and the most radical type of military confrontation?

The nuclear age is too dangerous a time for such simplistic solutions. Admittedly, great and dangerous discretion now lies in the hands of the executive. But the executive, unlike the Senate, is at least accountable for its mistakes. Moreover, would the Senate have avoided the mistakes Fulbright believes occurred in Viet Nam or would it have supported a declaration of war in 1965 had that been the only alternative then to withdrawal? With the experience of Viet Nam behind it, is the executive likely to engage in another major intervention soon in any case? And, after a lapse of five or more years, will the Senate remain the same watchdog it is today—particularly if Viet Nam should be taken over by the Communists?

The executive refused to countenance armed intervention in Viet Nam in 1954, largely as a consequence of the experience of Korea. By 1961, this had largely been forgotten. The greater danger, even from the senator's present perspective, lies in his mechanical proposals for the control of the executive branch of the government. These would produce unimaginable rigidities in our foreign policy, would be exceptionally inadequate in guerrilla wars and small-power confrontations, and would invoke exceptional danger in crises that might involve nuclear powers in confrontation.

Numerous polls have demonstrated that the American public soon wearies of limited wars that are fought for limited objectives. On those occasions on which we did intervene, the senator's proposals would re-enforce the public impulse for military escalation and total victory. They would sharpen rather than mute alternatives. They would lead to American retreats and then to overreactions. They would minimize the prospects for creative statesmanship and cater to the most simplistic of minds. In that advice lies the prospect of catastrophe.

Perspectives for Policy

Are there any general perspectives the government can apply in developing policy? If it cannot successfully plan in detail for the long run, and this writer does not believe that it can except in certain technological areas, it can keep in mind certain general ideas concerning the kind of world it is seeking to develop or alternatively the kind of world it is seeking to avoid. A fortress America world, for reasons given earlier, would seem to this writer a moral and political disaster greatly to be feared. A totalitarian-dominated world would be equally a disaster: the obverse face of the same coin. The greater the autonomy of the other areas of the world, despite the diminution of American influence that would result, the better and more compatible the world would be with American values. To the extent that only a united Europe can play an adequate major role in a future world, it seems appropriate to encourage such a development. The conditions for such unity do not exist in most other areas of the world, although China and Japan may each have sufficient strength to play reasonably autonomous roles in the world of the future.

Much of the rest of the world must be in some relative position of dependency. It would be most compatible with the values of the United States if international institutions could be developed for at least some important areas of activity that mitigated this dependency and re-enforced autonomous roles for these nations. To the extent that such dependency is not avoidable, the United States should encourage developments within areas and within particular countries that at least improve the capacity for autonomy of the citizens or nationals of the areas or countries. It is overly relativistic and indeed patronizing to view democratic institutions as inconsistent with the cultures or capabilities of other peoples. Perhaps their circumstances preclude democratic development at the present time and perhaps they even resist to some extent democratic developments. But then neurotics try to maintain their neurotic patterns to preserve the secondary but costly gains inherent in them. This is not to say that the forms of representation must be the same everywhere or that cultural or aesthetic or moral values must be identical. It does say that individuals of other nations, or of other races, or of other cultures are as inherently capable from a biological standpoint of exercising individual autonomy as are Americans and that political institutions that preclude this or that foreclose the possibility of such developments for the future are bad. Where other important interests do not preclude this, they should be opposed by the United States.

Toward an American Empire

Although on first sight the goal of an American empire will seem strange or even wrong, there is in the universalistic American value scheme something that might drive us to create a worldwide empire that is nonimperialistic and democratic. Some instrumental reasons might reinforce the movement toward such a goal. We need bases abroad to maintain our capacity for rapid military intervention. It is extremely important that these bases should not have any of the tinge of colonialism that the American bases in Okinawa, Japan, and the Philippines have.

Is there a better way to secure such bases than by expansion of the American nation? Australia, for instance, might be frightened that under some circumstances it might be deserted by the United States. So it might; it cannot hope under near-term circumstances to develop an adequate nuclear force of its own. Why should not Australia and New Zealand join the United States? Perhaps some day Israel might diminish in its nationalism and understand that its institutions manifest many of the same values as American institutions and that its safety might be best protected and its values best implemented in a more organic relationship with the United States. Some day the Philippines might retreat from the nationalism that is rising in those islands today. If in the meantime a more just social order has been created so that the present oligarchic character of the country does not serve as an impediment, the Philippines might remember its long history of association with the United States and desire to return as an equal member of an American nation.

If a universal organization such as the United Nations does not serve as the focus for a developing democratic world order, it is not inconceivable that an expansionary American nation might accomplish much of this task more successfully and with better fidelity to American national values that are ultimately truly universal values. We now lack the vision and the sense of mission that is required; in any event, much of the impetus will have to come from other nations, lest the growth seem an American imposition. But must these prerequisites always be lacking?

The principles of political philosophy underlying the American experience are genuinely universal. When they receive adequate expression in the United States through appropriate education and enlightenment, their spread might become a "natural" phenomenon. It is far from inevitable; but the idea of an American millenium is rooted deeply in the fundamental values of our Declaration of Independence. Perhaps our mission remains only to be discovered by ourselves.

Notes

1. This has been conceded even by the sceptical *New York Times*. See, for instance, the story by Terence Smith, "Pacification in Rural Vietnam Making Big but Fragile Gains" (October 16, 1969).
2. *New York Times* (February 3, 1970).

8 Freedom in History and in Politics

There is an old philosophical debate as to whether man's choices are free or are fully determined. It it true, and no reasonable man would question this, that a number of constraints upon freedom of choice do exist. The only such constraint recognized by Hobbes is physical constraint. A man bound to a post by iron chains is not free to leave that spot, according to Hobbes, but a man threatened by weapons is free to disregard the danger and to move. Although there is a sense in which we are absolutely bound by physical constraints, few of the actual physical constraints absolutely preclude contrary action. A Houdini could slip out of his chains, while another individual paralyzed by fear might remain unable to elude the constraint imposed by a toy gun. Still other individuals might be so constrained by habituation, perceptual delusion, moral fanaticism, or strategic inhibitions that their behavior in given types of situations becomes completely stereotyped, predictable, and uniform. Looked at from the obverse perspective, some individuals may appear to themselves to be able freely to choose from among alternatives; other individuals may have the oppressive sense of being completely constrained either by external circumstances or by internal inhibitions.

Some, at least, of the classic philosophers defined freedom as the recognition of necessity, by which they meant that man was free when he acted in harmony with his own nature. Others responded that this freedom was an illusion if it followed that man's actions were products of his biological being and of his social and psychological upbringing. Choice was an illusion, because man was constrained to do that which he was psychologically motivated to do and those who understood the motiva-

---

This chapter is reprinted from *Ethics* (July 1969, pp. 275-287) by permission of the publisher.

tions could predict the actions. Others questioned what use free-dom might be if use of it did not respond to a man's character and nature, for if it were not related to these in what sense would the action "belong" to the man?

In both the case of determinism and that of indeterminism, then, freedom might appear an illusion. In the one case, the act would be determined by circumstances, by constitution, and by upbringing; in the other case, the action would be the product of chance or of accident and thus unrelated in any meaningful way to choice. In the one case, freedom is the working of inex-orable necessity; in the other, freedom lies in the chance attri-tion from the norm produced by the flux of events in a complex world. In the one case the world is completely ordered; in the other the world contains surds that deviate from any statable rule and that produce discrepancies between class and individual. Yet an accident, or a deviation from a rule, is always an event that eludes control, and it therefore, although free in this sense, is a restriction on the freedom of the chooser. Thus the philoso-phy of Charles Sanders Peirce, or the earlier one of Heraclitus, which includes chance and accident, would seem on superficial examination to exclude freedom as much as fully deterministic worlds.

The difficulty with such discussions is that they occur at such a high level of abstraction that they do not distinguish between different kinds of systems. A railroad train may be said to have two degrees of freedom because it can move only backward or forward along the track. It cannot travel off the track or even onto other tracks for which the rails have not properly been set. A bus has many more degrees of freedom, for it can be driven on-to any existing road and even across some surfaces that are not roads. An amphibious vehicle can travel on the ground and in the water as well. It thus has a degree of freedom that the bus does not have. An automatic lathe has the freedom only to pur-sue a preset schedule of operations. Industrial equipment con-taining negative feedback has the capacity to reset or reschedule operations if certain deviations in the external environment are noted by the indicators of the system. An ultrastable machine has the capacity to change its mode of response to the environment by correcting its own internal programs if feedback indicates that its scheduled mode of operation for variations in the environment produces unanticipated and undesired results. The lower animals have a freedom to respond to psychological considerations that is not possessed by machines. Man has a freedom to respond to intellectual and to moral considerations. Two men may be said to differ in their degrees of moral freedom if one of them is incapable of adapting moral rules to circumstances and the other is capable of this. The former has lost the capacity to use negative feedback in this important area of activity. He thus may be said to have reduced freedom, a condition often, although not invariably, accompanied by consistent internal feelings. The psychopath, on the other hand, adjusts to circumstances not by adapting moral rules but by disregarding them. He has lost his capacity for moral action and has thereby reduced his freedom in a quite different way from that of the moral fanatic.

In our usage, freedom is related to the capacity for and the quality of action of different kinds of systems. Freedom is related to the types and numbers of responses the system has available for any environment, to its capability to use negative feedback, and to its possession of ultrastable or multistable capabilities. This usage is much closer to the classical definition of freedom as necessity than might at first appear to be the case.

Freedom is a relational concept and not an absolute concept. Freedom thus has restraint and constraint as its reciprocals. As the quality of the freedom becomes extended and complex and multifarious, so does the quality of the system of constraints and restraints become extended and multifarious. The freedom of a ball to roll in any direction is dependent on its globular shape. The freedom to act morally depends upon a framework for and a capacity for moral choice. Thus just as the freedom to roll is inconsistent with a square or rectangular shape, so is the freedom to act morally inconsistent with immoral or amoral character or nonmoral constitution. Every freedom requires a set of consistent constraints. These constraints are not merely limitations on the specified types of freedoms but are the very grounds for their

existence. That they are inconsistent with other modes of existence and with their particular freedoms, whether greater or
lesser or of a higher or lower mode, is tautological. The quest
for absolute freedom of revolutionaries and of anarchists is a
romantic and illogical attempt to recapture infantile feelings of
omnipotence. The quest for Godhead or for absolute freedom on
earth is a disguised death wish, as was so clearly pointed out by
Hegel, for in the historical world, if not in the fantasy world,
freedom is always related to constraint.

Closed and Open Systems

In part at least the confusions surrounding the subject of freedom
stem from failures to distinguish between closed and open systems and among choice, prediction, and retrodiction. Every prediction partaking of the character of law is made in terms of a
closed system. As Peirce pointed out, we cannot know whether
the laws of physics may not be changing. The world system is
open; our predictions are made entirely within the framework
of closed and bounded theories, models, or systems, or whatever
other term one prefers to use.

Knowledge concerning the world is always ineradicably
limited. Knowing is always a stage removed from the known;
the knowing self observes the known but is not itself known. Although any act of observing may itself be relegated to the realm
of the known by raising the level of examination or of knowledge,
there is ineluctably a metalevel at which one knows and is not
known. At the simplest and most general level of the distinction
between subject and object there is always a subject that is not
itself part of the knowledge equation. Although a subject may
observe itself or be observed by another subject, the metalevel
of subjectivity is never entirely brought within the realm of the
known.

Thus, even apart from uncertainty principles and the problems arising from measurement error, the world is never inherently a completely knowable phenomenon. Of course, matters do
not have to be pushed to this extreme, for it is also the case that

theoretical depth is purchased at the price of the restriction of the variables considered in a theory; depth of knowledge is pursued by increasing the number of variables external to one's theories or propositions that may affect behavior. Increasingly, as one moves from simple subjects the individual as an item of knowledge departs from the uniformity that would be imposed by putatively lawful formulations. Increasingly, surds and novelties assert themselves.

Yet to call these surds and novelties free creations would be to confuse their lack of predictability with their degree of freedom. Conversely, to assert that the predictable is unfree is to confuse its predictability with its degree of freedom. Would we assert that an unpredictable mutation is a freer act (it is, of course, not an act at all but an occurrence or event) than a predictable act, for instance, an honest man's refusal to steal money?

The freedom of a "free" action depends on the choosing and not on the choice. Our subjective awareness of freedom is an awareness that accompanies the act of choosing. Retrospectively the act may appear even to the chooser as completely determined. And so it may be, except that in the act of choosing, the display of alternative ends and of alternative means reveals the scope and range of the decision framework and therefore acquaints the chooser with the array of alternatives that he is physically and biologically and perhaps even socially and psychologically free to choose from, although perhaps constrained upon deeper examination by intellectual or moral considerations to merely a single one of the alternatives. As the choice is made, the range of alternatives is increasingly narrowed until finally reduced, often to one only. Yet, to make the choice less determined, as in the case of the ass torn between two bales of hay, where the choice may depend upon a number of accidental considerations having little or nothing to do with the healthful or aesthetic qualities of the food, such as closeness to or original attention to one of the bales, does not increase the freedom of the chooser. On the con- circumstances, it appears as externally constrained and less sub- trary, to the extent that the choice depends upon such accidental ject to freedom of choice. Where these external constraints or considerations are almost evenly balanced and dominant, the chooser does not feel free; he feels ambivalent and imprisoned by external circumstances. The higher or greater freedom of man is more fully made manifest the more his decisions rest upon the ultrastable reasoning processes, both intellectual and moral, and the less they depend upon fortuitous external, physical, or physiological constraints.

The undetermined type of freedom that we appear to have during the process of choosing arises from the contemplation of choice independently of the parameters that constrain it. Thus, the apparent freedom to steal of the honest man arises from contemplation of the act of acquiring money. "I could steal this money and purchase those things that I need or want," he thinks, "if it were not for my moral code." "I could do my enemy in if I did not have to tell a lie." "I could climb that rope if I were less tired." "I would eat that ice cream cone, as I am tempted to do, except that I wish to lose weight." Each of these statements reveals how, in the process of choosing, an end is considered in the absence of given constraints and then rejected as the appropriate constraint is recognized. Moreover, most of these acts are physically possible and thus may be committed if the motivation to do so is strong enough. Thus, "I ate the ice cream cone although I knew it was bad for me." "I stole the money although I knew it was wrong and did injury to others." Yet most people who commit such acts usually do not feel free; they rather feel themselves in the grip of a powerful emotion over which they lack ego control. In both sets of cases, the action is determined by the, at least momentarily, strongest motivation. In both, it is the closure of the open system as it was contemplated during the act of choosing that produces action. But in the latter set, and not in the former, the action is controlled by inputs from outside the ultrastable regulatory subsystem of the human system that dominate it. Another form of this phenomenon arises when a rigid superego controls the ego process. In neither case do individuals usually feel free.

Predictions and Retrodictions

Both historical predictions and retrodictions have to cope with the nature of the uncertainties arising from the open character of the historical process. Both predictions and retrodictions involve uncertainty. Thus, in the oft-used example of Cortés' third expedition to Baja California, it is sometimes argued that although it would not have been predictable that Cortés would have made the third expedition on the basis of his ambition, it is retrodictable that it was his ambition that led Cortés to the third expedition. This assertion is false. It was surely not predictable that Cortés' ambition would have led him to the third expedition, unless, of course, one also were able to fill in all the other circumstances and conditions that led to the choice. At best one might have predicted that Cortés would have been led to exploration or perhaps alternatively to armed conquest. On the other hand, the retrodiction that Cortés was led to the third expedition by ambition is at best credible. His characteristic of ambition is consistent with an activity such as the third expedition. Ambition, however, is not necessarily or clearly the motivation that led to the discovery. Prior to the third expedition, the known datum consists of the characteristic of ambition. The consequences of the ambition remain open. With respect to the retrodiction, we start with the third expedition. We find a credible motivation for the expedition in Cortés' known ambition. But it is only knowledge of the outcome that gives rise to false confidence in the known personality characteristic as the cause. Just as other discoveries or other self-assertive activities might have been predicted from Cortés' ambition, so other motivations or causes might be hypothesized for the known third expedition. In the prediction, the anterior event is known and the posterior inferred. In the retrodiction, the posterior event is known and a known anterior characteristic asserted as the cause. Although the retrodiction has at least two knowns, it is primarily a form of mental habituation that leads us to transform the certainty of the posterior event into the high likelihood that the known anterior characteristic functions as cause in a satisfactory explanation.

There is too much that we do not know and that we probably cannot know with respect to complex events and human motivations to view retrodictions as essentially different from predictions.

Historical explanation sketches almost invariably depend upon perspectives which are poorly articulated. A sketch of an explanation involves a choice of evidence from an almost unlimited array of potential evidence. Even the best of historical explanations are so selective in the use of evidence that they barely escape caricaturing the events they are designed to explain. Our interpretations of the evidence are themselves subject to doubt. Our weaving of the strands of evidence into an explanation sketch is too complicated in the case of complex events for us to examine the logic of relationships and the structure of inference in detail. It is only in the roughest and most precarious form that we know how our conclusions are related to our assumptions. We employ generalizations in interpretation that may be wrong, misunderstood, or misapplied. We deal with partial accounts only partially understood.

Even the most plausible interpretations of events constitute but a fragile house of cards ready to collapse at the first strong wind. Often a single piece of unexpected information may force us to revise or even to reverse the most convincing interpretations. Even the most solid evidence may serve to support a contrary hypothesis when re-evaluated in the light of other evidence or new hypotheses. To illustrate how fragile our hypotheses may be and how fragile the conclusions for policy we derive from them, consider such a typical event as the Czechoslovak coup of 1948. Did Russia plan the coup as early as 1944 or 1945? Even were we to discover documentary evidence that Russia did in 1944 or 1945 plan a subsequent coup, it would not follow inexorably that the later coup occurred because of the earlier plan. Even the discovery of a document written in late 1947 or early 1948 calling for the coup to implement an earlier plan of 1945 would not preclude the possibility that the coup was decided upon for entirely different reasons, but that it was rationalized in terms of earlier decisions because of a human motivation to project a continuity not present in the events themselves.

The firmest proof that the coup was decided upon for immediate reasons pertaining to the state of the world in early 1948 could not be used to demonstrate that an American reaction, based upon an interpretation that assumed that the coup was merely the culmination of a plan initiated in 1945, was an irrational or improper response to the circumstances of the coup. Nor could the discovery of proof that the coup was the fruit of a long-prepared, careful plan prove the rationality and reasonableness of an American response based upon a similar conception of the coup. Prudential responses to events may be based on interpretations that are less probable on the basis of available evidence than alternative hypotheses. Yet acting on a less probable hypothesis may deserve the characterization of "prudent" if acting on the alternative hypotheses entails greater risks. Moreover, the complicated relationship among prudential interpretation, motivation, knowledge of one's own motivation, and so forth, involves a feedback process that may be very difficult if not impossible for the historian to disentangle.

There is a tendency, perhaps ineluctable, given the needs of human beings for orientation in the world, to impose upon the pattern of events hypotheses whose unilinear dimensions deny the possibility of novelty and emergent levels of organization. Thus, with respect to the Soviet bloc, for instance, theories of permanent purges alternate with those of progressive societal changes toward freedom or even, in some cases, toward democracy. The intellectual difficulty of such theories lies not in the incorrectness of either, for either may turn out to be fortuitously correct, but in the almost casual assignment to reality of a prediction that pertains only to a model, whether implicit or explicit, that neglects many of the variables that will affect the real world outcome and that is blind to the sports that produce novelty.

It is amazing how often overly simple models are offered as conventional wisdom even in the face of contrary evidence. Thus, for instance, the Kennan-Fulbright thesis proposes that the way to produce favorable change in the Soviet bloc is to be friendly to individual bloc countries and to aid them. Yet

Yugoslavia broke with the Soviet bloc in 1948 during the period when American hostility toward Yugoslavia was even greater than its hostility toward the Soviet Union; China broke with the Soviet Union during a period in which American hostility toward China was greater than toward the Soviet Union; Rumania developed autonomy during a period in which American citizens were not even permitted to travel to Rumania; Poland, of all the Communist bloc nations, has been the most retrogressive since 1956, and it has been the recipient of large amounts of American aid and friendship.

The Kennan-Fulbright thesis is usually buttressed by the seemingly commonsensical argument that the advocated policy provides Communist governments with alternatives. But what kinds of alternatives does it provide them with? Did American aid perhaps reduce the Polish need for increased economic productivity, for the consensus underlying such productivity, and therefore for less repressive measures? Did acceptance of American aid increase the political need to stress Communist orthodoxy? Did American aid reduce internal opposition by showing American support for the regime, thereby removing a leadership incentive for reform? These questions, and numerous others that could be asked, suggest that at least some historical generalizations are based upon models, whether implicit or explicit, that **are so simplified that they are worthless for any purposes of extrapolation. They assert a simple determinism in the world** not warranted by any existing evidence. As guides to action, they circumscribe multistable freedom of choice in a thoroughly dysfunctional fashion. Those who have the responsibility for making decisions in the world cannot afford to assume a high degree of control over a determined and predictable simple world; such a world does not present itself in the historical realm. Decisions cannot simply be deduced from formulas; multistable self-regulation is a more complex process.

Freedom and Its Dysfunctions

To the extent that freedom can be regarded as multistable self-regulation at the rational and moral levels of analysis, majority rule or rules of equality in politics would merely be means toward the attainment of such ends. Although procedures are enormously important, for liberties are maintained in the interstices of procedures—a datum of social and political life not understood by the New Left—the concept of freedom as multistable self-regulation is basically substantive. The concept therefore suggests that, to the extent that equality is desirable, it should be obtained by leveling upward rather than by leveling downward and that, to the extent that a choice must be made between freedom and equality, the preservation of freedom somewhere in social and political life is preferable to equality. Freedom as multistable self-regulation implies that it is achieved not by the mere satisfaction of desires, as in a prototypical welfare state, but in the self-regulating attainment of desired ends. In this sense, both the pampered sons of the rich and the products of the dregs of the slums may be deprived of large areas of personal freedom through a process of education or acculturation that deprives one of the need of, and the other of the capability for, behaving freely.

The attempts by totalitarian governments and by supporters of the New Left to legislate or to coerce the moral beliefs of the general population involve (not necessarily conscious) attempts to destroy freedom of the individual, to suppress the diversity of life, and to force social and political processes within the world to conform to sets of narrowly chosen tenets: the moral equivalents of simplistic historical theories. Stasis, absolute freedom, and absolute death meet at Kelvin zero, at which all motion stops.

In Thomas Mann's *Magic Mountain*, the intellectual duel between Herr Naphta and Settembrini is a clash between opposing schemes for death, which differ from each other only in their intellectual guise. Peeperkorn, who ignores this dialogue but lives, represents the life principle that breaks through all attempts to impose rigid logical structures upon the world. Mann, however, achieves no synthesis, for Peeperkorn lacks the degree of intellectual control which is necessary for operating in the world and for recognizing that degree of order that temporarily exists and without which life would be impossible.

Individual freedoms exist, but they are relative and constrained by necessities. Order and disorder, freedom and rule, structure and process, are obverse faces of a common existence in which freedom can increase and reach higher levels of performance as the world becomes increasingly complex. Man's neuronic and biological structure provides the framework within which multistable moral and rational self-regulation are possible. The psychopath and the obsessive-compulsive are opposite dysfunctions of self-regulating systems. Both dysfunctions diminish the freedom of multistable systems, one by removing that framework of order within which freedom has meaning and the other by increasing the level of order to the point where all choices are uniformly determined regardless of environmental differences. Thus freedom too has its left and its right deviations. Self-regulation, the cybernaut, is a helmsman or steersman who must navigate the narrow route between the Scylla of absolute disorder and the Charybdis of absolute stasis. Order and disorder, freedom and control, are polarities bound in a symbiotic nexus, false opposites whose meanings are reciprocally revealed and whose limitations are overcome developmentally through appropriate synthesis in complex systems.